Extending

Knowledge in Practice

Primary
Mathematics

Extending

Knowledge in Practice
Primary
Mathematics

Alice Hansen

LearningMatters

First published in 2008 by Learning Matters Ltd.

British Library Cataloguing in Publication Data
A CIP record for this book is available from the British Library.

ISBN: 978 1 84445 0541

Cover design by Topics. Text design by Code 5 Design Associates Ltd
Project management by Deer Park Productions, Tavistock
Typeset by PDQ Typesetting Ltd, Newcastle under Lyme
Printed and bound in Great Britain by Cromwell Press Ltd, Trowbridge, Wiltshire

Learning Matters
33 Southernhay East
Exeter EX1 1NX
Tel: 01392 215560
info@learningmatters.co.uk
www.learningmatters.co.uk

Contents

The Author

Alice Hansen is a Principal Lecturer in Primary Mathematics Education at the University of Cumbria. She has taught extensively at primary level in England and abroad. Alice has particular interests in how children construct geometrical definitions, the design of mathematical tasks and the use of ICT to enhance mathematics teaching and learning.

Introduction

This book has been designed to help you identify how your mathematics subject knowledge and pedagogical knowledge support each other in order for you to become a better teacher of mathematics. Through case studies, a number of mathematical aspects will be considered. These cover some of the Early Learning Goals (DfES, 2007c) and a range of Programmes of Study in Key Stages 1 and 2 of the National Curriculum for Mathematics (DfEE, 1999). However, they are arranged in chapters according to the strands of the Primary Framework for Teaching Mathematics (DfES, 2006). These case studies are drawn from a wide range of year groups, from working with young children in nursery settings to working with more able children in Year 6. Other case studies focus specifically on relevant and interesting research that covers an important part of children's mathematical development. Accompanying each case study is a discussion aimed at developing your pedagogical and subject knowledge while it highlights the subject knowledge that the teacher requires in order to teach the objectives. Where appropriate, consideration is also given to how the teacher's subject knowledge developed while working with the children.

Although the book is set out in this way, it is essential to consider case studies from year groups other than the one(s) you are directly planning for. In most cases the discussion that ensues relates to a wider audience than the teachers of the specific year group in the case study and therefore the ideas that you find throughout the chapters can be adapted for most attainment levels.

Throughout the book you will see a number of cross references, shown by this symbol in the margin. These will help you to find other places in the book where similar aspects are being discussed. The high number of cross references demonstrates how the areas of the Early Years Foundation Stage, National Curriculum and the Primary Framework for Teaching Mathematics are interrelated, and how you cannot effectively teach one objective in isolation. One way to be able to make meaningful links between these areas of mathematics is to have good subject knowledge.

In addition to the case studies and the discussion, you will find sticky note reminders scattered throughout the chapter. These are useful prompts for your own subject knowledge, links to curriculum content or related reading/research for you to follow up if you require more information. There are also links to further reading to support your pedagogical knowledge and your subject knowledge of the aspect of mathematics being discussed.

This book aims to help you develop your mathematical subject knowledge and pedagogical knowledge so that your confidence in teaching mathematics develops, thus improving the learning and mathematical development of the children in your care.

What is the difference between mathematical subject knowledge and mathematical pedagogical knowledge?

Shulman (1986, 1987) defined three categories of teacher knowledge on which many have based their research into mathematical knowledge. These are: subject matter content knowledge (*the amount and organisation of knowledge per se in the mind of the teacher*), pedagogical content knowledge (that *goes beyond knowledge of subject matter per se to the dimension of subject matter knowledge for teaching*) and curricular knowledge (*the full range of programs and materials designed for the teaching of particular subjects and topics at a given level*) (Shulman, 1986, p9).

Many others have also considered the knowledge that teachers require to teach mathematics (Morris, 2001). For example, Ball and Bass (2000) identified the connections between mathematics content knowledge and teaching in what they termed 'mathematics knowledge for teaching'. They explained how this involved two elements, both 'common' knowledge (which any educated adult should possess) and 'specialised' knowledge (the knowledge of teachers) (Ball et al., 2005). What is clear from the research is that there are a number of elements that interrelate to enable teachers to effectively develop children's mathematical understanding. Whatever the labels different researchers assign to these, within this book the edges of the elements have been intentionally blurred in order to discuss the most appropriate aspects within the chapters more effectively, without being constrained by discrete (and sometimes artificial) groupings.

Do I really need good subject knowledge to teach mathematics well?

For the last 25 years the subject knowledge of teachers and student teachers has been a focus of government and initial teacher educators and it has recently become embedded within the Professional Standards for Teachers (TDA, 2007a). Indeed, *if teaching involves helping others to learn, then understanding the subject content to be taught is a fundamental requirement of teaching* (Aubrey, 1997, p3). Within initial teacher education the current focus on developing students' subject knowledge is evident. For example, it is a requirement for Qualified Teacher Status that student teachers pass their numeracy skills test (TDA, 2007a) and the TDA currently funds subject knowledge booster courses for students entering PGCE teacher training (TDA, 2008).

Research by Rowland et al. (2001) demonstrated that secure knowledge of mathematics (including and extending beyond the areas of the primary curriculum) is strongly linked with more competent mathematics teaching in student teachers. In addition to this, they found that poor subject knowledge was connected to less competent teaching.

Ball et al. (2005, p16) remind us that *although many studies demonstrate that teachers' mathematical knowledge helps support increased student achievement, the actual nature and extent of that knowledge – whether it is simply basic skills at the grades they teach, or complex and professionally-specific mathematical knowledge – is largely unknown.*

While subject knowledge plays a significant role in shaping the quality of teaching, it will be clear to you as a student or newly-qualified teacher that there are many factors that impact on your mathematics teaching. Indeed, *teaching performance is highly constrained and mediated by factors other than their subject content knowledge* (Rowland et al., 2001), such as the need to 'pass' a placement, the expectations of the mentor/class teacher and the available resources.

What if I am already confident in my subject knowledge?

Morris (2001, p41) worryingly demonstrates that confidence in mathematical subject knowledge does not necessarily correlate with accurate mathematical knowledge. In her study of initial teacher training students Morris identified that many of them were *overconfident in their mathematical ability, rating their confidence as high when unknowingly giving an incorrect answer*. Some, even after instruction, were adamant that their answers were correct. This is concerning because it is likely that teachers who are unaware of their own errors and misconceptions will teach these to the children they work with.

The Training and Development Agency (TDA) identifies continuing professional development as *a key factor in creating a dynamic, professional school workforce* (TDA, 2007b, p1). Indeed, through the Professional Standards for Qualified Teacher Status, student teachers are required to: *reflect on and improve their practice, and take responsibility for identifying and meeting their developing professional needs (Q7a)* (TDA, 2007a, p8). Within the Professional Standards, it is clear that *all teachers should have a professional responsibility to be engaged in effective, sustained and relevant professional development throughout their careers and all teachers should have a contractual entitlement to effective, sustained and relevant professional development throughout their careers* (TDA, 2007a, p4).

Fujita and Jones (2006, p129) point out the complexity of the issues involved in developing subject knowledge, *especially since the context in which teachers gain their own mathematical knowledge, and the form of teacher training (pre-service and in-service) they receive can be so varied, not only across countries, but also within particular countries*. This book provides a resource for you to be fully involved in your mathematical subject knowledge professional development throughout your initial teacher training and into your career.

How can I develop my mathematical subject knowledge while I teach?

Kafai et al. (1998) answer this well. In their paper on how both teachers' and pupils' mathematical enquiry can be developed in particular learning environments, they state:

> *Teachers who successfully implemented a new model of teaching based on the development of children's mathematical thinking, not only*

integrated the development of children's thinking into their existing knowledge structures, but also restructured their knowledge so that the principles underlying the new model drove the organisation of their knowledge ... But the key becomes how knowledge becomes integrated and organised for the teachers, and how teachers make connections between knowledge of children's thinking, knowledge of the mathematics, *knowledge of pedagogy and how* this knowledge organisation plays out in their classrooms.

(Kafai et al., 1998, p152)

Doerr and English (2003) examine how features of tasks supported teachers' knowledge as their pupils undertook tasks. Through working with their pupils on the tasks, the teachers were able to develop their knowledge and understanding of the mathematical content, their pedagogy (including listening, observing and questioning) and how the children learnt. Based on these principles, Doerr (2006) reported the practice of a teacher who developed her teaching through listening and responding to her pupils' alternative solution strategies. In doing this, the teacher developed a sophisticated understanding of her pupils' thinking. This process developed her subject content knowledge and subject pedagogical knowledge.

Margolinas et al. (2005) also consider how teachers' subject knowledge and processes of learning in the classroom develop. They believe that through reflecting upon their observations and interactions with pupils and their work, teachers develop their 'observational didactic knowledge'.

Common to all these studies is the reflective teaching undertaken by the teachers and student teachers, based on the work of the children in their classes. Throughout this book you are invited to reflect upon your own subject knowledge and to consider how you might develop your own mathematics content and pedagogical and curricular knowledge.

1
Using and applying mathematics

Introduction

Historically, using and applying mathematics has been an aspect of teaching that teachers have found difficult to plan for and implement. However, through adopting an approach that fully integrates the notions of use and application in all areas of mathematics it is possible to help children to learn mathematical content through effectively integrating problem-solving, reasoning and communication into mathematics lessons.

One approach to learning mathematics is modelling, which is championed by researchers such as Doerr and English (2006) and Lesh and Zawojewski (2007). English and Watters (2005) and English (2006) highlight how children of primary school age are confident problem-solvers, who are able to develop their own models to solve complex problems that are presented to them. This chapter inherently offers models that children can use to support their use and application of their mathematical knowledge.

FURTHER READING
Read more about developing children's mathematical thinking in Drews and Hansen (eds) (2007) *Using resources to support mathematical thinking*. Exeter: Learning Matters.

In this chapter we will look at five aspects of using and applying mathematics.

1. *Understanding patterns and relationships*. How does knowledge of patterns and relationships underpin mathematics learning and teaching? How can teachers use questioning to develop understanding of this? This includes a case study about a group of Y1 children looking at pattern in colour.

2. *The development of early symbols*. The importance of symbols in mathematics is discussed. The case study and ensuing discussion consider how young children develop their own mathematical notation that leads to numerals. Children's understanding of the equals sign is introduced also.

3. *Using diagrams as a tool to solve problems*. How can diagrams be used flexibly to solve problems and generalise powerful ideas? This includes a Year 4 case study about children using diagrams to solve a problem about football scores.

4. *Multi-step problems and BODMAS*. What is BODMAS? How is it used to help us calculate the answer? What is the difference between an arithmetic calculator and a scientific calculator? This includes a Year 5 case study about children using these two types of calculators

5. *Using formulae and describing the general term*. How do children develop their understanding of algebra? What place might spreadsheets have in developing this further? The case study looks at a Year 6 class who use spreadsheets to handle a large amount of data to solve a problem that was real to them.

1. Understanding patterns and relationships

Patterns and relationships can be found wherever we look in the world and they are fundamental to all mathematics and many other disciplines. Indeed, finding and understanding patterns and relationships helps children to make sense of the world, and making connections within aspects of mathematics and between mathematical topics helps them to learn mathematics more effectively.

CASE STUDY: PATTERN IN COLOUR AND NUMBER (YEAR 1)

Context
In this case study, Simon is working with a group of Year 1 pupils. They have a box of colourful interlocking cubes and are making linear patterns with two colours of their choice.

Curriculum Content
National Curriculum Key Stage 1
Pupils should be taught to:

Ma2.1a: communicate in spoken, pictorial and written form, at first using informal language and recording, then mathematical language and symbols.

Ma2.2b: create and describe number patterns, explore and record patterns related to addition and subtraction, and then patterns of multiples of 2, 5 and 10 explaining the patterns and using them to make predictions, recognise sequences...

Primary Framework Year 1
Describe simple patterns and relations involving numbers or shapes; decide whether examples satisfy given conditions.

Describe ways of solving puzzles and problems, explaining choices and decisions orally or using pictures.

Task
While you are reading this case study, think about how Simon is using questioning to elicit discussion about their patterns.

Simon:	Look at this pattern I have created. Who can describe it to me?
Raheema:	It goes blue, blue, yellow, blue, blue, yellow.
Simon:	That's right, Raheema. I've joined two blue cubes together, then placed a yellow one next. I repeated that pattern. Would you like to continue it, James?
James:	(*Continues the pattern blue, blue, yellow, but ends with blue, blue only.*)
Simon:	What can you tell me about your pattern, James?
James:	Well, it goes blue, blue, yellow and on like that.
Simon:	Would anyone like to say anything about James's pattern?
Mika:	It is really long! (*All laugh.*)
Simon:	Yes, it is really long. Does anyone else want to tell us something about it?
Raheema:	It needs another yellow one to finish it.
Simon:	Why?

Raheema:	Because you did blue, blue, yellow. Blue, blue, yellow is the pattern. And he finished with just blue, blue. It should be blue, blue, yellow.
James:	(*Adds another yellow cube to the pattern.*)
Simon:	Can you see what Raheema means, James?
James:	Yes.
Simon:	I can see two other patterns made by children in the group that are quite similar to James's pattern. Can anyone else see them?
Kelly:	Mine!
Simon:	Why?
Kelly:	Because mine goes black, black, pink, black, black, pink. And yours is like that too. (*She takes James's pattern and puts it alongside hers.*) See? (*Kelly points to the cubes in both patterns.*)
George:	Mine is too! Look! (*He puts his alongside the other two patterns.*) (*Further discussion occurs*)
Simon:	Well done everyone. Now that we have looked at these patterns, I want to focus on James's pattern. What is the first colour?
All:	Blue
Simon:	And the second?
All:	Blue
Simon:	And the third?
All:	Yellow.
Simon:	OK, we're going to play a game now. I'd like you to close your eyes and tell me what colour you think the fourth cube is.
All:	Blue.
Simon:	Well done. What about the, hmm, sixth one?
All:	(*Some children glance at the pattern Simon has in front of him. Others give the answer.*)

Extending subject knowledge

Using questioning to elicit mathematical discussion

Mathematical discussion is essential to developing an understanding of what is being learned (Yackel and Cobb, 1996; Edwards, 1991). Raiker (2007) highlights the need for teachers to be aware of the language they use with children and to use appropriate, precise mathematical vocabulary, but also be aware of how important is the careful introduction, explanation and repetition of vocabulary.

One method of ensuring the above is to use effective questioning skills that 'incorporate proper use of silence' (Amin and Eng, 2003: 147). Raiker (2007) raises two crucial issues about questioning. The first is that teachers on average wait less than one second for an answer to a question they have posed. The second is that most of the questions that teachers pose are closed. However, if teachers use open and higher-level questioning, the wait time needs to be increased because of the time children require to process the question. Studies (such as Tobin, 1987) show that higher quality responses come from increased wait time.

Using your own subject knowledge to develop the children's understanding of patterns and relationships

In the case study, Simon used his knowledge of how children develop early notions of algebra (patterns and relationships) by employing the following strategies.

- He limited the number of colours that the children could use to two in order to focus their attention on creating manageable patterns that they could easily discuss.
- He linked the colour pattern that the children were confident discussing with numbers, helping them to create a mental image representing the multiples of the three times table.
- He asked a number of open-ended questions to find out what the children knew about pattern.
- He drew the children's attention to the similarities and differences between some of their patterns.
- He highlighted for the children that a pattern repeats.

FURTHER READING

The QCA website has information on how to use questioning further in *Assessment for Learning* (AfL).

2. Understanding notation: the development of early mathematical symbols

The QCA (1999: 3) reinforces the need for children's mathematical development to begin with mental calculation and that *recording of one form or another should take place regularly and is an essential part of learning and understanding*. They explain that the role of the teacher includes ensuring *that learning is reinforced and that children move progressively from informal to more formal methods of recording when they are capable of understanding the underlying mathematical processes*.

CASE STUDY: THE RESEARCH OF MARTIN HUGHES AND OTHERS (EYFS AND KS1)

Context

This case study provides a brief overview of the seminal work of Martin Hughes.

Curriculum Content

The Early Learning Goals
Problem solving, reasoning and numeracy:

Recognise numerals 1 to 9.
Use developing mathematical ideas and methods to solve practical problems.

National Curriculum Key Stage 1
Pupils should be taught to:

Ma2.1a: communicate in spoken, pictorial and written form, at first using informal language and recording, then mathematical language and symbols.

Task

While you are reading this case study, think about your experience of working with young children. To what extent have you considered how they are developing their mathematical thinking through their 'scribbles'? As a teacher, what is your role in developing children's mathematical thinking through notation?

Martin Hughes' work in the 1980s challenged people's perspectives about children's early mathematical knowledge and their acquisition of mathematical symbols. In his book, *Children and Number*, Hughes (1986) shows how the written symbolic representations that children create for themselves are more meaningful to them than the taught conventional symbols.

Hughes' research involved him asking three- to six-year-old children to place small cubes into containers and to mark on the lid something that would help them to remember at a later date how many were in the container. He found that while some children made idiosyncratic marks that they were unable to later understand, a large number of children were able to interpret their marks at a later date. This seminal work made teachers aware that children made their own marks to represent mathematical concepts so that they could support 'emergent mathematics' in the way they were already supporting 'emergent writing'.

Others have emulated Hughes' study (Montague-Smith, 1997; Pound, 1999; Vandersteen, 2002) and found similar results. However, Munn (1997) was critical of the findings in her (similar) study, suggesting that the children wrote something which was a memory aid rather than something that demonstrated the total number of cubes in the box. Regardless of the reason for the mark-making, it is clear that the records made were a representation of the cubes in the box, communicating a mathematical meaning (Vandersteen, 2002).

Carruthers and Worthington (2005) have built on the foundations that the work of Hughes and others have undertaken. Unlike the research above, which was based on clinical tasks, their data was collected over a decade and involved the analysis of nearly 700 samples of children's work in homes, nurseries and classrooms where they have worked themselves. The samples were also collected from a range of tasks, from child-initiated to adult-led sessions where the children chose what to record themselves.

Extending subject knowledge

Carruthers and Worthington – taking Hughes' work further
Carruthers and Worthington (2005) acknowledge the importance of children making their own marks (they identify five different forms of symbolic representation themselves), but they explain that the mathematical choices children make while writing is 'enlightening and more complex' than the marks themselves. This is because the marks that are made tend to be produced on published worksheets or during a teacher-led session. Through their analysis of nearly 700 samples of children's work, they have designed a taxonomy of children's 'mathematical graphics'. The taxonomy includes five dimensions. While it is not hierarchical, the first four must be in place prior to the fifth.

FURTHER READING
To find out more about Carruthers and Worthington's work, go to http://childrens-mathematics.net/

1. **Early play with objects and explorations with marks**
   Here, Carruthers and Worthington highlight the need for a 'fluidity' for children moving between playing with objects and making marks.
2. **Early written numerals**
   In this dimension, children refer to their marks as numbers and make numerals that have meaning to them.
3. **Numerals as labels**
   Children use number in their environment as symbols or labels. They understand that different numerals might be used in different contexts.
4. **Representations of quantity**
   Children represent particular quantities that they may or may not have counted. They may be things that they can or cannot see.
5. **Early operations: development of children's own written methods**
   This contains five stages of development, which move from 'counting continuously' through to 'mental methods supported by jottings'.

Using your own subject knowledge to develop the children's understanding of mathematics through mark-making

It is crucial for teachers to be able to plan for a range of activities appropriate for children to be able to make their own marks. It is surprising to note that Carruthers and Worthington (2005) were unable to find Early Years settings and classrooms other than their own to undertake their research because of the highly interventionist nature of the teaching in the classrooms they visited. In those classrooms, children were not being encouraged to undertake their own mark-making but rather were expected to be following the notation required by the teachers.

Chapter 3 has an annotated example of a child's piece of mathematical mark-making.

By reflecting on the extent to which children's mathematical development is enhanced through their own mathematical graphics and mark making, planning for appropriate opportunities for this to happen is an essential tool for the teacher.

Children's understanding of the = sign

You can read more about these types of questions in Chapter 4.

For a number of years, teaching has appeared to reinforce for young children that the = sign is an operator. For example, Baroody and Ginsburg (1983) explained how a Grade 1 pupil, on explaining the = sign, stated: *It means it would add up to, and whatever the answer was, you'd put it down* (p198). They also explain that children find it very difficult to accept statements such as $12 = 4 + 8, 7 + 2 = 5 + 4$ and $6 = 6$. Additionally, they outline that children find questions such as $\square = 4 + 7$, $11 = \square + 7$ or $11 = 4 + \square$ more difficult to solve than questions such as $4 + 7 = \square$ because of the emphasis on reading the equation from left to right.

Jones and Pratt (2007) suggest that the reason for this narrow understanding of the = sign is due to the pencil-and-paper algorithms that are carried out in schools. Additionally, calculators reinforce the same left to right reading of the sum. Jones is exploring the affordances that computer microworlds offer to enable children to develop their understanding of the = sign as an equivalence (see Jones and Pratt, 2006).

3. Using diagrams as a tool to solve problems

Dougherty and Slovin (2004) demonstrate how children working at National Curriculum Levels 1 and 2 are capable of using algebraic symbols and generalised diagrams to solve problems. Their research demonstrates a positive impact on children's mathematical development through the simultaneous use of models, representations and symbols. This challenges more common-place practice, where physical models are introduced first to children and from this, representations and finally symbolic representations are developed.

CASE STUDY: FULL-TIME SCORES (YEAR 4)

Context
In this case study, Sara has set her pupils a task that is encouraging them to use diagramatic representations to support their mathematical thinking and to communicate their reasoning.

Curriculum Content
National Curriculum Key Stage 2
Pupils should be taught to:

Ma2.1g: use notation diagrams and symbols correctly within a given problem.

PNS Framework for mathematics
Year 4: Represent a puzzle or problem using number sentences, statements or diagrams; use these to solve the problem; present and interpret the solution in the context of the problem.

Task
While you are reading this case study, think about how the different diagrams encourage logical reasoning.

Sara has explained to her class that a full-time football score from a game she watched at the weekend was 2–3. She wants to know if the children, in pairs, can consider what the half-time score could have been. She encourages the children to use any method of recording that they want to, to represent their thinking. Below are some examples of the pupils' work that were discussed at the conclusion of the lesson.

FURTHER READING

Toyn (2007) wrote about this task and interactive whiteboards in Chapter 8 of Drews and Hansen (eds) *Using resources to develop mathematics thinking.* Exeter: Learning Matters.

A

	0	1	2	3
0	0-0	1-0	2-0	3-0
1	0-1	1-1	2-1	3-1
2	0-2	1-2	2-2	3-2

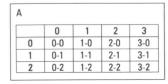

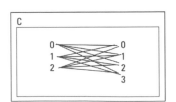

B

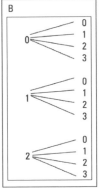

Extending subject knowledge

Using diagrams to empower children's abilities to generalise

The majority of the children in Sara's class began to list all the possible scores they could think of. This was an ad hoc method and so Sara encouraged her pupils to think of other ways to record their work more systematically.

Once the pupils began to understand the methods that some of the children had devised, they were able to use the strategies to efficiently identify other possible half-time scores from other full-time results.

Another advantage of encouraging children to record using diagrams is that they can use the same strategy in other contexts to solve other problems. For example, the diagrams above could be used to identify how many ways I could pair my green hat, scarf and gloves with my red hat, scarf, gloves and coat.

4. Multi-step problems and BODMAS

BODMAS is an acronym used to remind us of the order in which operations should be undertaken in arithmetic or algebraic equations. Depending on which country you live in, an alternative acronym might be used (see Table 1.1).

Table 1.1 Order in which operations should be undertaken

Acronym	Country of use	Order of operations			
		1st	2nd	3rd	4th
BODMAS	United Kingdom Australia New Zealand	Brackets	Orders (exponents, square roots, etc.)	Multiplication/ division	Addition/ subtraction
BEDMAS	Canada	Brackets	Exponents	Multiplication/ division	Addition/ subtraction
PEMDAS	United States	Parentheses	Exponentiation	Multiplication/ division	Addition/ subtraction

CASE STUDY: 'THIS CALCULATOR IS WRONG, MISS!' (YEAR 5)

Context

In this case study, the pupils in Shirley's class are undertaking multi-step word problems. Shirley has given the children a number of word problems to select from. Their task is to identify what calculation is required of the two-step problem, then work out the solution to the problem.

Curriculum Content

National Curriculum Key Stage 2
Pupils should be taught to:

Ma2.1b: break down a more complex problem or calculation into simpler steps before attempting a solution; identify the information needed to carry out the tasks.

PNS Framework for mathematics
Year 5: Solve one-step and two-step problems involving whole numbers and decimals and all four operations, choosing and using appropriate calculation strategies, including calculator use.

Task
How would you explain to Year 5 children how the calculator came up with a different answer from the one expected by the pupils?

> Andy was saving his pocket money because he wanted to buy a new computer game. Each week, he received £4.00 as pocket money, but he also did a number of additional jobs around the house which meant he earned a further £6.00 each week.
>
> After three weeks, he had saved enough money for his game. How much did he save over the three weeks?

Tariq: This calculator is rubbish, Miss.
Shirley: Pardon, Tariq?
Tariq: It won't do the right answer. This calculator is wrong!
Shirley: Show me what you mean.
Tariq: Well, I worked out that he got £4.00 from his pocket money and then another £6.00 doing his jobs. That's £10.00, right? And then you times that by the three weeks and that's £30.00. But when I do it on the calculator: 4 + 6 × 10 ... the answer is 64! This calculator is wrong!
Shirley: How do you think that the calculator worked out an answer of 64?
Tariq: It did 6 × 10 first which was 60 and then added the 4, but that's wrong because he got ten pounds for three weeks.
Shirley: You are right, Tariq. The calculator doesn't know what the word question is about, so it isn't taking into consideration the context that you are. Therefore, it is calculating the multiplication before the addition.
Tariq: Why?
Shirley: The calculator is using a particular order of operations, where it calculates the multiplication and division first, then the addition.
Tariq: But how can I get it to do it the way I want to do it?
Shirley: The calculator would add the four and the six first if you put brackets around them. (*She goes on to write (4 + 6) × 3 and shows how following the order of BODMAS produces a different answer to following the number sentence through from left to right.*) Anyway, you didn't even need a calculator to check that answer!
Tariq: I know! (*He laughs.*)

You can read more about calculators being used in Chapter 4.

REMINDER
There is a calculator on your computer under 'Accessories'. You can change the type of calculator it is by going to 'View' and selecting either 'Standard' or 'Scientific'.

Extending subject knowledge

Arithmetic and scientific calculators

Many calculators that are used in primary schools are arithmetic calculators (or four function calculators: Jones, 2003) which will calculate a solution as the numbers and operations are entered. On these calculators, the answer to the problem discussed above will be 30. However, children often bring their own calculators to school, or upper Key Stage 2 classes might have invested in calculators that automatically take into consideration the order of the operations. These are termed scientific calculators and will calculate the 6×3 first, unless brackets are used (or the equals button is pushed) when entering $4 + 6$.

5. Using formulae and describing the general term

Schliemann et al. (2003) explain how until recently there has been much research demonstrating that children struggle with algebraic reasoning. They identify four particular areas that have caused difficulty. These are limited understanding of:

- the equals sign;
- letters standing for variables;
- answers that contain a variable (e.g. '$3a + 7$');
- how to solve problems where a variable exists on both sides of the equals sign.

FURTHER READING
You can read more about Schliemann et al.'s work at http://earlyalgebra.terc.edu/

Chapter 7 makes reference to 'human graphs' for helping young children make sense of data.

However, recently a number of studies have been carried out that challenge these assertions. Schliemann et al. (2003) undertook a study with children in Grades 2–4 that led them to argue that *given the proper conditions and activities, elementary school children can reason algebraically and meaningfully use the representational tools of algebra*. One example of a task undertaken by the children began with the statement, 'Maria has twice as much money as Fred'. The children formed a 'human graph' and this helped them to discuss the relationships between the variables, make generalisations and draw conclusions.

Ferrara et al. (2006, p237) explain how the historical development of aspects such as our number system, written language, methods of calculation and algebraic notation gave humans powerful tools to support their mental capacity and to record and share information. The most recent of these 'representational infrastructures' (Kaput et al., 2002, cited in Ferrara et al., 2006, p237) to have been developed is technology. This development has built on the previous tools, offering two new opportunities for humans. These are that *human participation is no longer required for the execution of a process, and that access to the symbolism is no longer restricted to a privileged minority of people, as it was in the past* (p237).

Wilson et al. (2005) undertook a longitudinal study which looked into the ways in which using appropriate tasks with a spreadsheet might help children to develop their algebraic understanding. They discuss how the majority of Year 7 (11–12 year olds) interpreted a cell (e.g. A2) as 'any number' but still interpreted variable cells within the context of the problem.

CASE STUDY: SPEEDING CARS (YEAR 6)

Context

Ellie was taking the register with her class when Jason walked in crying and grazed. Upon asking what had happened, Jason informed his teacher that he had fallen off his bike as a large lorry had overtaken him on the main road. There were general comments of concern from the class members and general agreement that the vehicles 'always speed down that road'. Ellie and the class decided to test this hypothesis.

Curriculum Content

National Curriculum Key Stage 2

Pupils should be taught to:

Ma2.1b: break down a more complex problem or calculation into simpler steps before attempting a solution; identify the information needed to carry out the tasks.
Ma2.1c: select and use appropriate mathematical equipment, including ICT.

PNS Framework for Mathematics

Year 6: Tabulate systematically the information in a problem or puzzle; identify and record the steps or calculations needed to solve it, using symbols where appropriate; interpret solutions in the original context and check their accuracy.

Task

While you are reading this case study, think about how the pupils are engaged because they see a purpose and use for their work. Reflect on the extent to which the tasks you design for your pupils have similar purpose and utility for them.

Ellie:	How do you think we could work out the speed of the cars going along the main road?
Oliver:	We could stop the cars at the start of the village and ask the drivers if we could go in the car with them, and then look at their speedometer when they go past the school to see if they are speeding. (*General laughter.*)
Ellie:	Hmmm … I think that we might have some difficulties with that one!
Oliver:	Yeah, the cars wouldn't speed when they know we're checking up on them.
Ellie:	Other ideas?
Sam:	We could work out a mile and then time how long it takes them to go one mile and that would be how many miles per hour.
Ellie:	That is an interesting suggestion, Sam. What do people think about that idea?
Martin:	It is good but we wouldn't know when the car finished the mile because the road has a bend in it and we wouldn't see it.
Ellie:	Good point, Martin. So, could we adapt Sam's suggestion to make it manageable?
Martin:	Yeah, we could do a shorter distance, like half a mile, or quarter of a mile.
Ellie:	That is a good idea, Martin. Instead of working in miles, how about we think about metres, instead? We all know that there are

1,000 metres in a kilometre, so we can still work out whether or not the cars are speeding by using kilometres per hour instead of miles per hour. But what will we need to know, in order to work out the speed?

Extending subject knowledge

The use of spreadsheets to support manipulation of large amounts of data

After general discussion about ideas, Ellie was able to draw out of her pupils' ideas the formula that Speed= Distance/Time. They also worked out that they could use their trundle wheel to work out a distance of 100 metres along the main road outside the school. They knew that 100 metres was one tenth of a kilometre. They also deduced with Ellie's assistance that the distance they were measuring was 0.1 of a kilometre so the Speed = 0.1/Time (in hours). Two of the gifted and talented children in the class were able to calculate that the time in hours could be shown as a fraction with a denominator of 3,600 because there were 3,600 seconds in an hour (60 seconds in a minute × 60 minutes in an hour).

After collecting the data using a stopwatch (Ellie checked with the head teacher that this would be acceptable and ensured she had enough adult support with her), the children returned to the class and entered the data together.

Because the children were more confident with discussing speed in miles per hour, they added another column (E in Figure 1.1 below) to calculate miles per hour. They used a conversion aid on the Internet to convert kilometres to miles. The children found that one kilometre is equal to 0.62136 miles and used that to create a formula that calculated the speed in miles.

Ellie added a final column (F) using an IF function on the spreadsheet to enable the children to see at a glance the results of their data.

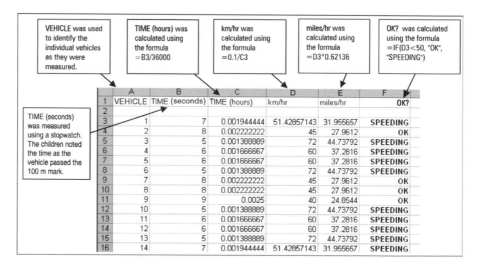

Figure 1.1 Data for calculating speed of cars.

The majority of the pupils were able to understand how the formulae entered into the speadsheet enabled them to see the results of their data. They acknowledged that their method of data collection was not particularly accurate and they tended to round up the seconds. This is another example that demonstrates Dougherty and Slovin's (2004) research of children being capable of using algebraic symbols to solve problems. Ellie differentiated her lesson by assigning different tasks to pupils of different attainment.

Using your own subject knowledge to develop the children's understanding of formulae

Ellie was confident in her mathematical subject knowledge in the following areas: She was able to:

- convert from metres to kilometres and vice versa;
- manipulate simple formulae (Speed = Distance/Time) to calcuate the data required;
- utilise the spreadsheet effectively for the children to gain the most useful data they required.

Using meaningful situations to develop children's mathematical learning

Ellie was also able to use a critical incident in the classroom to encourage the children to use and apply some challenging mathematical ideas to solve a problem that was real to them. She had tapped into an area that interested them and they wanted to find out what mathematics they needed to use to help them solve their problem. In doing so, the task had a *purpose* for the children – they were also able to see how they could use mathematics (the *utility*) to solve their problem. Ainley et al. (2006) explain how it is necessary for both purpose and utility to be present in effective task design. In their work on the Purposeful Algebraic Activity project, Bills et al. (2006. p46) analysed a range of children's work and concluded that *the role of purpose in the students' work was seen as vital, not just as a form of motivation but as material for the construction of meaning for variables and for algebraic notation and expression*.

2
Counting and understanding number

Introduction

Being able to count has been of the utmost importance to the development of human-kind in history. Nowadays, counting forms an essential foundation for all aspects of mathematics. For example, 'counting on' is the first strategy used when learning to add (see Chapters 3 and 4 for more on this). Counting also helps us to make sense of our number system by ordering not only the whole numbers but all other numbers such as positive and negative integers, decimals and fractions. By understanding and utilising the relationships between numbers (say, between decimals and fractions), we can calculate mentally more efficiently and accurately.

In this chapter we will look at four aspects of counting, comparing and ordering numbers, and describing relationships between them.

1. *Counting*. How do children learn to count? How does knowledge of the principles of counting help us to support their understanding of counting? This includes an Early Years Foundation Stage case study about a group of three-year-olds helping Teddy learn to count.

2. *Zero as a place holder*. What is the difference between numbers and numerals? Where did our numerals come from? Why is zero such an important digit? This includes a Year 2 case study about children writing numerals and thinking about zero as a place holder.

3. *Fractions*. What kind of numbers are fractions? Are there different ways of thinking about fractions? This includes a Year 5 case study about a teacher setting problem-solving questions involving fractions.

4. *Percentages*. What are percentages? How do you calculate percentages mentally? Is there an easy way to calculate VAT? This includes a Year 6 case study about the class using derived facts to calculate percentages of whole numbers.

1. Counting

Learning to count

As adults we take counting for granted. However, in 1978 Rochel Gelman published with her husband a seminal article about the underlying principles of counting (Gelman and Gallistel, 1978) which really made teachers think about how complex learning to count really is. They found five principles of counting that must be followed before becoming adept at counting. These are divided into two groups. The first three are the 'how to count' principles and the remaining two are the 'what to count' principles. Below is a brief overview of these principles.

How children count

The one-one principle

In order to be able to count, a child needs to be able to understand that each object in a set should be counted once ('partitioning') and that once an object has been counted, it cannot be counted again. In addition to this, a label or tag should be applied to that object, and the label can be used only once ('tagging').

The stable order principle

The labels or tags given to each object need to be in a stable, repeatable order.

The cardinal principle

The final tag in any set gives the cardinal number of that set (i.e. the total number of objects in the set). Because the cardinal principle can develop only after the one-one and stable order principles, it is often more difficult for children to use and it develops later.

What children count

The abstraction principle

A child knowing that he is five years old or that he has his tea at five o'clock appears different to that child from counting five counters, and so the abstraction principle raises the question about what is countable to a child. As adults we understand that any object, real or imagined, can be counted. If a child does not fully appreciate how a counting procedure can be used to represent number then they have not grasped the abstraction principle.

The order-irrelevance principle

This principle is concerned with a child knowing that it doesn't matter what order the objects in the set are counted, the final label always provides the cardinal number. A child who demonstrates this principle is able to count an object as a 'thing' rather than associate it as a particular number. This demonstrates how the abstraction principle is inherent within the order-irrelevance principle.

To summarise, a child may be able to recite a list of the numbers, say from one to twenty, but not be able to apply the principles. In situations such as this they are not demonstrating a real understanding of counting. Likewise, it would be possible for a child to be able to count using the principles but not use the traditional labels we use. In order to illustrate this latter point, Gelman (1978) shares examples from other languages (for example a range of East African cultures whose labels are rooted in everyday practice, and Greek or Hebrew where their alphabets are used) where counting is undertaken effectively.

CASE STUDY: HELPING TEDDY TO COUNT (EYFS)

Context:

In this case study, Marissa is working with a group of three-year-old children. She uses her Tiny Ted puppet to help them to think about their counting.

Curriculum Content

The Early Learning Goals

Problem Solving, Reasoning and Numeracy: Count reliably up to ten everyday objects.

Task

While you are reading this case study, think about which principles of counting Marissa is encouraging the children to think explicitly about. What advantages do using a toy or puppet bring in sessions such as this?

Marissa:	Today I have brought a friend to nursery with me. His name is Tiny Ted. Can you all say hello to him?
Children:	Hello, Tiny Ted.
Marissa:	Tiny Ted wanted to come along today to learn how to count. He is quite good at his counting but he needs some help sometimes. Will you help him practise his counting?
Children:	Yes!
Marissa:	Can you count how many bricks are on this table, Tiny Ted?
Tiny Ted:	One, two, three, five, six
Children:	No!
Marissa:	What do you mean, 'No'? Can you help Tiny Ted?
Tiny Ted (with Children):	One, two, three, four, five.
Tiny Ted:	Six! There are six bricks!
Children:	No! There are five! One, two, three, four, five! There are five!
Marissa:	How do you know there are five, Shamim?
Shamim:	Because it's one, two, three, four, five. See? There are five. Not six.

FURTHER READING
You can find Rochel Gelman's chapter 'Counting in the preschooler: what does and does not develop' as a download on her website, at: http://ruccs.rutgers.edu/faculty/Gelman/

Extending your subject knowledge

The principles of counting in practice

Tiny Ted was able to demonstrate the one-one principle because he associated a name/label/tag (in this case one, two, three, etc.) to each object (in this case, brick) he counted. He knew not to count any object more than once and he also knew that once he had used one label, he shouldn't give that same label to a different object. In the above case study it is possible to identify two principles that Tiny Ted is struggling with. These are the stable-order principle (where Tiny Ted missed out the number four) and the cardinal principle (where Tiny Ted counted correctly to five but then suggested there were six bricks).

Using your own subject knowledge to develop the children's understanding of counting

In the case study Marissa was knowledgeable about the five principles of counting. She also understood that the children she was working with needed to be confident using the 'how to count' principles before they developed the 'what to count' principles.

Young children believe that adults (and in particular their teacher!) know everything. By using a toy, Marissa was able to present intentional errors to the children in a way that they felt completely at ease to challenge. The children were enthusiastic about helping Tiny Ted learn to count. By highlighting Tiny Ted's difficulties with counting Marissa was able to place the focus on her 'friend' – a toy which didn't know all the answers and in fact struggled with counting, something that the children also struggled with. By setting up particular scenarios that focused on the two principles she needed the children to develop, Marissa was able to question particular children in order to gain further understanding about learning to count and help them develop their understanding of counting.

You can read more about how young children create their own symbols in Chapter 1.

2. Zero as a place holder

The history of our numerals

We use the digits 0, 1, 2, 3, 4, 5, 6, 7, 8 and 9 in our number system. However, this has been a fairly recent innovation in humankind's history with these numerals only being consistently used in Europe since about the 1650s. Because some people call these numerals the Arabic numerals you might find it surprising to find that the Arabs actually called the digits Hindu numerals because they borrowed them from India perhaps 500 years before they ruled Spain and introduced them to Europe around 1000 AD.

> **REMINDER**
> Our base ten place value system is a **decimal** system because we have **ten** (using the prefix deci-, meaning ten) digits!

CASE STUDY: CAN YOU WRITE TWENTY-SEVEN? (YEAR 2)

Context
In this case study, Sharon is working with the whole class during the oral/ mental starter of the mathematics lesson. They are writing two-digit numerals on the board.

Curriculum Content
National Curriculum Key Stage 1
Pupils should be taught to:

Ma2.1e: use the correct language, symbols and vocabulary associated with number and data.

Ma2.2c: read and write numbers to 20 at first and then to 100 or beyond . . . recognise that the position of the digit gives its value and know what each digit represents, including zero as a place holder. . .

Primary Framework Year 2
Read and write two-digit and three-digit numbers in figures and words.

Task
What is the role of the zero in our place value system? Why does it have such an important role? Why do you think some children find it difficult to write numbers involving zero?

Sharon:	In today's starter we are reminding ourselves how to write two-digit numbers. What do I mean by two-digit numbers?
Shaun:	They are numbers that have two digits in them.
Sharon:	Thank you Shaun. Can you think of a two-digit number for us?
Shaun:	Twenty-seven, Miss.

> **FURTHER READING**
> Denise Schmandt-Besserat has written a wonderful picture book for older children called *The history of counting* (1999). Not only will it enlighten you and your pupils but it will enable them to see number and mathematics in a different and exciting way!

Sharon:	Yes, twenty-seven is a two-digit number. Can someone come and write twenty-seven on the board for us? Thank you, Sally.
Sally:	(*Writes 207 on the board.*)
Sharon:	What number have you written here, Sally?
Sally:	Twenty-seven.
Sharon:	Who thinks that Sally has written twenty-seven for us? (*A mixed response of hands goes up*)
Sharon:	I think we need some convincing, Sally. Can you circle the part of the numeral that shows us twenty, Sally?
Sally:	(*Circles the 20 of 207.*)
Sharon:	Can you put a line under the part of the numeral that shows us seven?
Sally:	(*Underlines the digit 7.*)
Sharon:	Now who agrees that Sally has written twenty-seven for us? (*Still a mixed response.*)
Sharon:	Who would like to come up and write the number two hundred and seven for us? Thank you, Michel.
Michel:	(*Writes 207 on the board.*)
Sharon:	Who can tell us something interesting about these two numerals?
Bart:	They look the same, but they shouldn't!
Sharon:	What do you mean, 'they shouldn't'?
Bart:	Well, that one (*pointing to the first numeral*) says twenty-seven but that one (*pointing to the second numeral*) says two hundred and seven so they're different numbers but they look the same!
Sharon:	You're right, Bart. They do look the same and they are the same number! Which number is not quite right?
Children:	Twenty-seven.
Sharon:	Why not?
Holly:	Because the twenty should just be a two, not twenty because that makes it two hundred then.
Sharon:	Do you understand what Holly means, Sally?
Sally:	No.
Sharon:	Explain it again for us please, Holly?
Holly:	Well, if you have twenty-seven it is just a two and a seven because you know that the two is really a twenty by where it is in the number.
Sharon:	(*Draws 27 on the board.*) Like this, Holly?
Holly:	Yes!
Sharon:	Holly, which numeral do you think shows us twenty-seven? This one (*points to 207*) or this one (*points to 27*)?
Holly:	(*Points to 27.*) That one.
Sharon:	Why, Holly?
Holly:	Because that one is two hundred and seven and that one is twenty-seven.
Sharon:	Thank you, Holly. Who can tell me how many tens are in twenty-seven?
Mike:	Two.
Sharon:	Yes, Mike, there are two tens in twenty-seven. (*Sharon goes on to model this to the children in two ways. First, she sticks twenty*

> red magnetic counters on the board, creating two columns of ten. She also sticks up seven blue counters in a column next to them. Sharon then uses place value arrow cards to show 27. She shows 20 on its own.) Now, how many tens are there in two hundred and seven?
>
> **Sam:** There aren't none.
>
> **Sharon:** Yes, there are no tens in two hundred and seven, well done Sam. How did you know that?
>
> **Sam:** There are two hundreds and seven ones but no tens.
>
> **Sharon:** Which digit in this numeral tells you that?
>
> **Sam:** The zero.

Extending your subject knowledge

FURTHER READING: Read pages 181–90 in I Thompson (2003) *Enhancing primary mathematics teaching*. London: Open University Press for more information on seeing place value as column value and quantity.

Place value: the framework of our number system

Recently Ian Thompson challenged teachers to think about how they teach place value. He warns that children are less likely to calculate with meaning if they are only exposed to place value as 'column value'. In order to be flexible and creative in mental calculation, Thompson (2003) explains how we also need to approach place value as a 'quantity value'.

In the case study above, Sharon did consider place value in these two ways: Firstly as a 'quantity value' (when she showed the counters) and secondly as a 'column value' (when she used the place value arrow cards and asked how many tens are in 27 and 207). She encouraged the children in her class to think about the numeral 27 in a range of ways, for example as 20 + 7, 2 tens and 7 ones/units.

Sharon's confidence in her subject knowledge about place value and about zero as a place holder was evident in her questioning of the children. She had planned for the likely difficulty the children might have with using zero as a place holder because she had observed some children in the previous lesson making similar errors when writing numerals. As a result she had a range of resources and questions ready to use.

Read more about the value of digits when multiplying and dividing by 10 in Chapter 3.

The history of zero

Zero is perhaps the most important digit in our number system because it represents the empty set. However, in history the notion of zero took a long time to develop. Imagine that when numbers were used to represent groups of objects, there was no need for a number to represent a non-existent group! For many thousands of years several great civilisations used numbers without zero. For example, the Babylonians used a base-60 place value system for over one thousand years without a zero. Instead, they relied on the context to help interpret the numerals. While this might seem absurd, we actually use context informally as part of our everyday lives often also. For example, we might be charged for a drink costing 'two forty' (£2.40) whereas we would know that the asking price of a house at 'two forty' would be £240,000.00.

Chapter 1 considers other aspects where context is important, e.g. in problem-solving.

How zero was introduced into our place value system

One historic civilisation to use zero was the Mayans. They used a base-20 place value system that included a zero as a place holder. But it was the Hindu-Arabic number system once again that introduced zero to Europe to a select few in around the eleventh century AD after being used in India since the sixth century. Earlier in this chapter mention was made about the Arabs introducing the Hindu number system into Europe when they ruled Spain. Much is also attributed to the Italian mathematician Leonardo Pisano (better known as Fibonacci) for popularising the Hindu number system and in particular introducing zero to Europe. Fibonacci wrote an encyclopaedia entitled *Liber Abaci* that became a school textbook for people studying mathematics. It was Fibonacci's intention that not only mathematicians use the Hindu number system, but all people in all walks of life because he saw the number system as a superior tool for calculating without an abacus. Eight hundred years after Fibonacci's original book was published, Sigler (2003) translated *Liber Abaci* from Fibonacci's original text. Here is an excerpt from Fibonacci's encyclopaedia explaining how he painstakingly brought the Hindu number system to Europe:

> *After my father's appointment by his homeland as state official in the customs house of Bugia for the Pisan merchants who thronged to it, he took charge; and in view of its future usefulness and convenience, had me in my boyhood come to him and there wanted me to devote myself to and be instructed in the study of calculation for some days. There, following my introduction, as a consequence of marvelous instruction in the art, to the nine digits of the Hindus, the knowledge of the art very much appealed to me before all others, and for it I realised that all its aspects were studied in Egypt, Syria, Greece, Sicily, and Provence, with their varying methods; and at these places thereafter, while on business, I pursued my study in depth and learned the give-and-take of disputation. But all this even, and the algorism, as well as the art of Pythagoras, I considered as almost a mistake in respect to the method of the Hindus (Modus Indorum). Therefore, embracing more stringently that method of the Hindus, and taking stricter pains in its study, while adding certain things from my own understanding and inserting also certain things from the niceties of Euclid's geometric art, I have striven to compose this book in its entirety as understandably as I could, dividing it into fifteen chapters. Almost everything which I have introduced I have displayed with exact proof, in order that those further seeking this knowledge, with its pre-eminent method, might be instructed, and further, in order that the Latin people might not be discovered to be without it, as they have been up to now. If I have perchance omitted anything more or less proper or necessary, I beg indulgence, since there is no one who is blameless and utterly provident in all things. The nine Indian figures are: 9 8 7 6 5 4 3 2 1. With these nine figures, and with the sign 0 ... any number may be written.*

What is the role of zero in our place value system?

Because we have only ten digits (0, 1, 2, 3, 4, 5, 6, 7, 8 and 9) that we use to represent all numbers, we rely on our understanding of place value to interpret the position of the digits to give us the size. For example, if we had nine objects in a set and we added three more to that set, we don't have a specific symbol to represent the number of objects present. Instead, we would exchange the 9 + 3 for a 12, showing that there was 1 ten and 2 ones:

If we added eight more, we would end up with 2 tens and 0 ones, represented as 20. If we did not use zero to hold the ones/units place, we would not be able to discriminate between 2 or 20, or even 200 or 2,000,000,000,000!

Children can find it difficult to understand the role of zero as a place holder when their first experiences of seeing zero in notation is in the numbers they are counting, such as 10, 20, 30 and so on. Having recited the label 'thirty' for the numeral '30' for some time, it is understandable to want to write 'thirty-four' as 304 (a 30 followed by a 4).

3. Fractions

Much research suggests that children possess an intuitive knowledge of the underlying aspects of fractions (see Kafai et al., 1998; Wu, 2002), particularly the notion of fair sharing (Streefland, 1991, 1993).

However, it is common for fractions to be narrowly-defined by adults as 'one number divided by another number'. While it is possible to find a fraction as a result of division of two whole numbers, this is only one way to consider them.

It is important to remember that a fraction is a number in its own right. It has its own place on a number line and can be represented by a decimal number. For example, ½ can be written as 0.5 and is found between 0 and 1 on a number line. Wu (2002) strongly believes that this really is the only definition that is required of a fraction and that all other meanings can be logically deduced from this.

Another common way of representing a fraction is as a part of a whole. For example, children are very familiar with having their apple cut in half or sharing a pizza so everyone in the family gets a quarter.

Similarly, it is possible to think about a fraction as comparing a subset and a whole set. For example, we might say, 'Half of the children in my class are boys' or 'One quarter of my salary goes on my rent'. This can also be referred to as a proportion.

Finally, we can use fractions to compare the sizes of two objects or two sets of objects. For example, we might say, 'My brother is half the height of my sister'. This can also be referred to as a ratio.

REMINDER
Rational numbers are any numbers that can be written as the ratio (see the link?!) of two integers, e.g. $^3/_4$, 1.75 and $^{-195}/_3$.

Irrational numbers are any numbers that can be written as decimals but not fractions, e.g. pi, e and $\sqrt{2}$.

FURTHER READING
Further explanation and illustrations of the ways to consider fractions can be found on page 22 in Mooney et al. (2007) *Primary mathematics: knowledge and understanding*, 3rd edn. Exeter: Learning Matters.

> ## CASE STUDY: PROBLEM-SOLVING WITH FRACTIONS (YEAR 5)
> ### Context
> *In this case study, Louise wants to encourage her pupils to use fractions in a range of contexts, so she has set up a variety of problems for them to solve in mixed-attainment groups of 3–4 children over one and a half lessons. Below are the cards she has given the groups. (The 'sharing time' refers to the 30-minute plenary she will have in the second lesson.) Over the two lessons Louise and her TA plan to have worked with all the groups on at least one challenge.*
>
> ### Curriculum Content
> <u>National Curriculum Key Stage 2</u>
> Pupils should be taught to:
>
> *Ma2.2d: understand unit fractions then fractions that are several parts of one whole, locate them on a number line and use them to find fractions of shapes and quantities.*
>
> <u>Primary Framework Year 5</u>
> *Express a smaller whole number as a fraction of a larger one; relate fractions to their decimal representations.*
>
> ### Task
> *In what way is each problem card expecting the children to consider/use fractions? What resources could you provide for the children to work through the questions? Can you complete the challenges? Why is it important for teachers and children to use fractions in a variety of contexts?*

Extending your subject knowledge

The challenge cards

The challenge cards (see opposite page) can be solved in a multitude of ways, however one suggestion for each is provided below. How did you get on?

Challenge 1

This problem can be solved by dividing each chocolate bar into four parts (creating quarters). This is done because there are four people sharing them evenly. If the quarters were then shared out one at a time, each person would get one quarter from the first bar, one quarter from the second bar and one quarter from the third bar. This would leave them with three quarters each.

It is possible to consider the problem as a division: 3 (bars) ÷ 4 (people) = ¾ .

Challenge 2

This encourages the children to think of fractions as numbers on a number line. This challenge gives them proper and improper fractions to consider. The children could use a calculator (if they need it!) to find out the equivalent decimal number. This might make the placement of the fractions more straightforward.

Challenge 1

Four people evenly share three chocolate bars.

How much of each bar do they get?

Make sure that you can explain your answer clearly to the class in sharing time!

Challenge 2

Order these numbers on the number line. Make sure everyone in your group agrees with where they are placed. You will be asked to explain why in sharing time!

⁹/₁₀   ½   ²/₃   ⁶/₄   ¼
²/₄   ⁵/₁₀   ²/₂   ⁴/₂

0   2

Challenge 3

In a box of 24 Smarties: 6 are red, 6 are blue, 5 are orange, 4 are purple, 3 are green.

What fraction of Smarties are: green? purple? a primary colour?

Make your own set of 12 objects to show: ¹/₄, ¹/₂, ¹/₃, ¹/₆ !

Challenge 4

How many different ways can you cut a rectangular cake to make enough equal pieces for 30 people?

Record your work to present to others in sharing time.

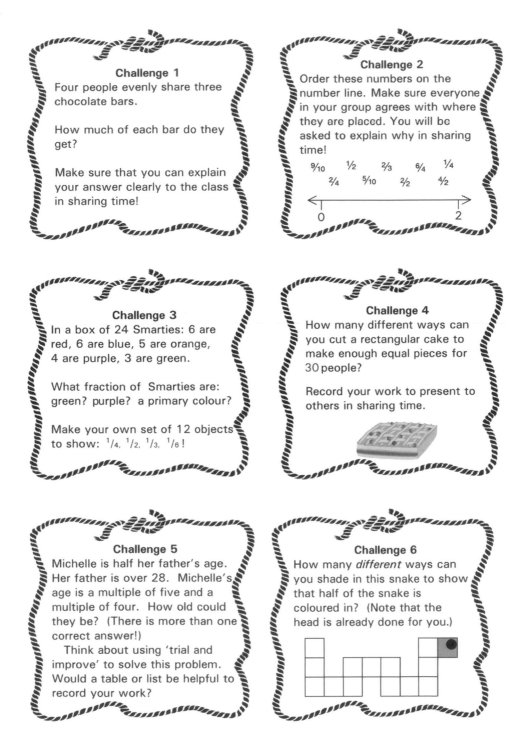

Challenge 5

Michelle is half her father's age. Her father is over 28. Michelle's age is a multiple of five and a multiple of four. How old could they be? (There is more than one correct answer!)
    Think about using 'trial and improve' to solve this problem. Would a table or list be helpful to record your work?

Challenge 6

How many *different* ways can you shade in this snake to show that half of the snake is coloured in? (Note that the head is already done for you.)

Challenge 3

This problem is encouraging the children to think of the coloured Smarties as subsets of the whole set, or as a proportion represented as a fraction. For example, the green Smarties are one eighth of the whole because $3 \times 8 = 24$.

Challenging the children to create their own set of 'objects' is particularly difficult if they are going to move away from colour. They could use their own erasers or leaves forming sets from subsets to make groupings of fractions.

Using a number like 24 (or 12) is good because it has a lot of factors. The factors of 24 are: 1, 2, 3, 4, 6, 8, 12 and 24 which makes it possible to create fractions with the same denominators.

Challenge 4

This challenge considers how fractions can be used to show part of a whole. The cake could simply be cut to give 6 rows and 5 columns because $6 \times 5 = 30$. However, one group in Louise's class went on to think about creating 3 rows and 5 columns (to make 15 pieces) and then cut the cake in half again through the centre where the (imaginary) cream filling was! More able pupils could be challenged to continue this pattern.

Challenge 5

This was a difficult challenge for some of the children because it involved a number of steps. It was considering fractions as ratios. Several of the groups in Louise's class started by thinking that if the father was 28 then Michelle was 14. They then realised that 14 was not a multiple of 4 or 5 and so moved on to find the first multiple of 4 and 5, which is 20. That provided one possible answer. Many children used the information about Michelle's age being a multiple of 4 and 5 to solve the problem. As a class during the plenary in the second lesson they agreed as a class that the possible answers could be 20:40 and 40:80. There was some discussion that a third could be 60:120 but how unlikely would that be!

Challenge 6

This challenge encouraged the children to think about the snake as a whole and find parts of it. Simply, the next six squares from the snake's head could be coloured. Alternatively, every second square could be coloured. In Louise's class some of the groups got carried away and began to shade half of each of the squares (and all the tail to balance it) to shade half. They then tried dividing the squares into quarters. This led to discussions on the second day about the infinite ways that a shape can be shaded to show a fraction.

Using and applying fractions in a range of contexts

Read more about calculating with fractions and decimals in Chapter 4.

Just as it is essential for children to be flexible in their approach to calculation with whole numbers, it is also essential that they feel confident calculating with fractions and decimals. We would expect children to be able to tell us a lot of things about the number 25 (such as: it is $100 \div 4$, $20 + 5$, 2 tens and 5 ones, 1 more than 24, 5 less than 30, etc.). Equally we should expect children to be able to understand fractions in the same way (for example, ¾ is: ¼ less than 1, $1\frac{1}{2} \div 2$, 0.75, ¼ + ½, 75%, ¹⁵⁄₂₀, etc.). This offers us and our children a far more efficient and effective route to calculation. By being aware of, and providing, a range of contexts in which children can use and apply their fraction knowledge we help to develop their understanding of fractions in a far more enriched way than a limited approach that focuses on only one or two representations.

The history of the word 'fraction'

Fraction comes from the Latin meaning 'to break' or 'a breaking in pieces'. It was first used mathematically around the fifteenth century, about the same time that **fracture** was used to refer to broken bones.

4. Percentages

What are percentages?

Understanding the root of 'per cent' helps us to make sense of what percentages are and how they are used in maths. Per cent comes from Latin (pro-centum) and means 'on hundred'. So, considering one per cent in this way gives us 1 on 100 (1/100), or one hundredth. Through this definition it is straightforward to identify the relationship between percentages, fractions, decimals, ratio and proportion. Table 2.1 points to the relationship between the ways of representing some percentages.

Table 2.1 Ways of representing percentages

Percentage	Fraction	Decimal	Ratio	Proportion
1%	1/100	0.01	1:99	1 out of 100
5%	5/100 (1/20)	0.05	5:95 (1:19)	5 out of 100 (1 out of 20)
10%	10/100 (1/10)	0.1	10:90 (1:9)	10 out of 100 (1 out of 10)
50%	50/100 (1/2)	0.5	50:50 (1:1)	50 out of 100 (1 out of 2)
75%	75/100 (3/4)	0.75	75:25 (3:1)	75 out of 100 (3 out of 4)
100%	100/100 (1/1)	1	100:0 (1:00)	100 out of 100 (1 out of 1)
150%	150/100 (15/10)	1.5	150:100 (15:10)	*n/a*

Read more about the relationships between fractions, decimals and percentages in Chapter 4.

A second representation, which better demonstrates the continuity of the numbers, is the number line:

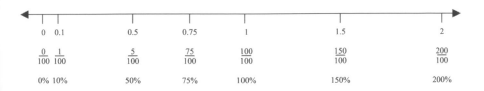

You will notice in the table above that it is not possible to write percentages higher than 100 as a proportion. Following the pattern, 150% would be written as the proportion 150 out of 100, which is invalid because they demonstrate parts of a whole.

Calculating percentages effectively and efficiently

Although having an understanding of percentage as 'on hundred' is helpful, it is also necessary to be confident in using the relationships between the representations when calculating. How this can be beneficial to calculating is explored in Chapter 4.

Calculating percentages using the rule of percentage as 'on hundred' works, but it can be very technical as can be demonstrated below:

35% of £300 could be calculated by:

$$\frac{35}{100} \times 300 \qquad\qquad \frac{35 \times 300}{100}$$

or:

$$0.35 \times 300 \qquad\qquad \frac{10{,}500}{100}$$

By utilising simple relationships such as knowing that 10% is one-tenth (which is very quick to calculate mentally), it is possible to calculate any percentage. For example, 35% of £300 can be calculated by finding 10% of £300 (which is £30) and then finding three times 10% to make 30% (£90). Finally 5% is found by halving the answer for 10% and adding it to the total (£90 + £15 = £105).

This method can be used to calculate Value Added Tax. VAT is 17.5%. We can find 17.5% by adding 10% + 5% + 2.5%. Can you see how each percentage is half of the previous one?

In the following section we look at an Upper Key Stage 2 class using the relationships of percentages described above to work out various percentage amounts of twenty-six.

CASE STUDY: USING DERIVED FACTS TO CALCULATE PERCENTAGES (YEAR 6)

Context

Zainub is a student teacher on placement in a Year 6 class. She has been looking at derived facts to calculate percentages of numbers with the class. The diagram below was drawn on the whiteboard during a whole-class discussion.

Curriculum Content
National Curriculum Key Stage 2

Pupils should be taught to:

Ma2.2g: recognise approximate proportions of a whole and use simple fractions and percentages to describe them, explaining their methods and reasoning.

Primary Framework Year 6
Express one quantity as a percentage of another; find equivalent percentages, decimals and fractions.

Task
What mental strategies are the pupils being encouraged to use to calculate the percentage values of 26?

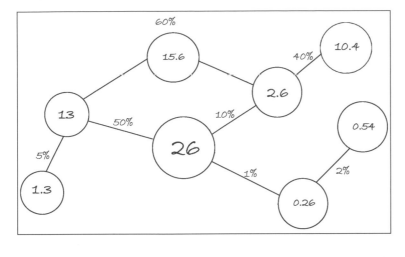

Extending subject knowledge

Exploring the relationship between percentage values
By using a spider diagram to record her discussion about the percentage values with the children, Zainub was able to represent for them the relationships between some of the key percentages. For example:

- The children knew that 50% was equivalent to half, so finding ½ of 26 gave 13. 10% was found by dividing 26 by 10 giving 2.6. These two totals were added together to find 60%.
- By finding 1% of 26 and then doubling it, the children were able to calculate 2%. Zainub also talked with the children about how doubling and doubling again could multiply a number by 4 when they looked at finding 40% using their knowledge of 10% to do this.
- By finding 50% and then one-tenth of that, the children calculated 5%.

By being secure in her own subject knowledge Zainub was confident in encouraging the children to calculate the percentage values flexibly. For example, she spoke to the children about other ways of calculating these percentage values (such as finding 1% and multiplying it by 5 to find 5%). Zainub used a constructivist approach to her teaching by helping the children to draw links between percentages, fractions and decimals.

3
Knowing and using number facts

Introduction

This chapter is concerned with many of the skills and strategies that are required for effective and efficient calculations, such as the quick recall of number facts, and being able to use and apply those skills and strategies appropriately. Gray and Tall (1994) explain that there are two aspects to answering a question such as 5 + 3. There is the *process* of adding the two numbers together and the *product* of adding 5 + 3. They report that 'more able' children are able to think flexibly between the process and the concept, using what they call a *procept*. They hypothesise that *the more able thinker develops a flexible relational understanding in mathematics, which is seen as a meaningful relationship between notions at the same level, whilst the less able are faced with a hierarchical ladder which is more difficult to climb* (Gray and Tall, 1994, p75). In their study they identified a 'proceptual divide' between the more and less able, where the less able are confined to process-orientated study while the more-able children are able to think proceptually: *It is as though the less able are deceived by a conjuring trick that the more able have learned to use* (Gray and Tall, 1994, p75).

In this chapter we will look at six aspects of recalling number facts and using and applying them appropriately.

1. *Finding one more and one less*. How do children build on their counting strategies to develop ideas of 'one more' and 'one less'? How can continuous provision and observation support children's mathematical development? This includes an Early Years Foundation Stage case study about a group of three-year-olds using a book as a stimulus and drawing their own representations of more and less. Analysis of a child's work is undertaken.

2. *Deriving facts*. How does deriving facts support pupils' calculation strategies? How can teachers help children to develop models and images to be able to derive facts? This includes a Year 1 case study about a child using derived facts to generate number bonds.

3. *The multiplication facts*. Why is knowledge of the addition, subtraction, multiplication and division facts essential to mental and written calculation? How might children learn the multiplication facts? How does the exploration of pattern within the multiplication facts help children to learn them? This includes a Year 4 case study about children exploring the digital roots of the multiples of the nine times table.

4. *Rounding*. What are the purposes of rounding? How does context support introducing the concept of rounding to children? This includes a Year 4 case study about a class visiting a football ground as a stimulus for learning about rounding and estimating.

5. *Factors and divisibility rules*. How can using factors and the divisibility rules support children in their calculations? How can display support mathematical development? How can common factors and multiples be found? How can Venn diagrams record this information? This section includes a Year 5 case study on finding factors.

6. *Multiplying and dividing by multiples of ten*. What misconceptions might children be led to if they just 'add two zeros' when multiplying by 100? How can music support children's learning? The case study in this section observes a Year 6 class discussing what effect multiplying and dividing by powers of ten has on the value of the digits.

1. Finding 'one more' and 'one less'

In Chapter 2 we considered how children learn to count. Fusion (1992) explains what happens, around the age of four or five, after children have learnt to count. She identifies two factors that come into play to decrease children's accuracy in their counting: they have internalised counting (saying the word silently and looking at the objects rather than touching/pointing to them), and they begin to put less effort into the process, believing it to be easy or even babyish. The implications for teachers, Fusion (1992, p62) believes, is to *accept counting in their classes so that it will not go underground and become more errorful* because *this counting is crucial for the construction of later more efficient addition and subtraction procedures*.

CASE STUDY: THE SNAIL AND THE WHALE (EYFS)

Context
In this case study, Victoria is reading The Snail and the Whale *(Donaldson and Scheffler, 2003) with a small group of three- and four-year old children in a pre-school. On the first page there are five seagulls in the sky and two seagulls sitting on rocks. This captures the interest of the children.*

Curriculum Content
The Early Learning Goals
Problem Solving, Reasoning and Numeracy: Find one more or one less than a number from 1 to 10.

Task
While you are reading this case study, think about which principles of counting Victoria is encouraging the children to think explicitly about. What advantages do these principles give?

Amelie:	(*Spontaneously counting the seagulls at the top of the page.*) One, two, three, four, five. (*Then pointing to the seagulls sitting on rocks.*) One, two. (*Then pointing to all seagulls.*) One, two, three, four, five, six, seven. There are seven.
Victoria:	Yes, there are seven birds. They are called seagulls. Five here and two sitting on these rocks.
Amelie:	I know.

Victoria:	What would happen if one of the seagulls flew away? (*Covers one of the seagulls with her hand.*)
Amelie:	(*Counts the remaining seagulls.*) One, two, three, four, five, six.
Victoria:	What if another one flew away, Cameron? (*Covers a second seagull with her hand.*)
Cameron:	There would be five left.
Victoria:	How do you know that?
Cameron:	Because that one would fly away next and there'd be five left. One, two, three, four, five.
Victoria:	Oh, I see. Which one might fly away now?
Stuart:	That one. (*Points to another seagull and covers it with his hand.*)
Victoria:	How many would be left if we had one less?
Stuart:	There would be those two there. One, two. And those two there. That makes one, two, three, four.
Victoria:	So, we had seven seagulls and three of them flew away and left us with those four there. What if one seagull came back? What if we had one more?
Cameron:	There would be five again. (*Moves Stuart's hand to reveal one of the flying seagulls.*) One, two three, four, five.
Victoria:	Good. Four seagulls, add one more, makes five seagulls. Show me five fingers. (*Counting on her fingers. The children join in.*) One, two, three, four, five. What if another seagull flew back?
Michelle:	There would be six. Look. Four there (*points to flying seagulls*) and two there (*points to sitting seagulls*). That is six.
Victoria:	Yes, there would be six seagulls, very good Michelle. So how many more seagulls would need to fly back to make seven seagulls again?
Amelie:	One more.
Victoria:	One. See, when that last one comes back there are seven again.

FURTHER READING
You can find similar counting activities for Reception to Year 3 children in the Models and Images CD-Rom from the NNS (2003). Ref no. DfES 0508-2003 GCDI. Available at: www.standards.dfes. gov.uk/primary/ publications/ mathematics/models _and_images_pack/ playing

Later that morning, Victoria brings some plastic birds to a table where Amelie, Victoria and Stuart are playing. They are invited to explore similar ideas, with the birds flying away and being hidden under a teatowel. She also provides some paper for the children to record their own pictures of the birds flying away and returning. Figure 3.1 shows Amelie's (aged 3 years 2 months) annotated picture of the seagulls.

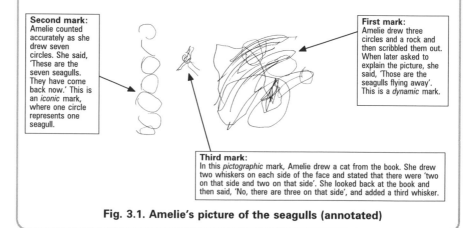

Second mark: Amelie counted accurately as she drew seven circles. She said, 'These are the seven seagulls. They have come back now.' This is an *iconic* mark, where one circle represents one seagull.

First mark: Amelie drew three circles and a rock and then scribbled them out. When later asked to explain the picture, she said, 'Those are the seagulls flying away'. This is a *dynamic* mark.

Third mark: In this *pictographic* mark, Amelie drew a cat from the book. She drew two whiskers on each side of the face and stated that there were 'two on that side and two on that side'. She looked back at the book and then said, 'No, there are three on that side', and added a third whisker.

Fig. 3.1. Amelie's picture of the seagulls (annotated)

Extending subject knowledge

Child-initiated activities and observation

Smidt (2005, p1) tells us that *observation is the best tool we have for understanding if and how children are learning*. She makes explicit the role of what she refers to as the 'thinking observer', and reminds us that *if we observe children attentively and thoughtfully we gain insights that are priceless when we start to think about learning and development* (p3). Additionally, the DfES (2007a, p2) reiterates that *carrying out regular observations is vital because it ensures that we put the child at the centre of our practice*. Ouseley and Lane (2006, p10) remind us to be mindful of the need for observation *to be as free of stereotypes and cultural assumptions as possible in order to avoid incorrect interpretations of what has been observed*.

In Chapter 1, the work of Carruthers and Worthington was mentioned with regard to mark-meaning. In encouraging the children to 'draw a picture or write about the seagulls flying away and coming back', Victoria was creating a 'fluid' environment that was allowing the children to manipulate the objects and record their ideas. Indeed:

> When teachers encourage children to decide how they will 'put something down on paper' and listen to what children say about their marks, they are provided with new insights into children's development. Children need to make sense in their own ways rather than colouring-in ours. And young children are very good at making their own sense through their own marks and symbols ...
>
> (Worthington and Carruthers, 2003, p23)

Amelie's graphics – analysis according to Carruthers and Worthington

Amelie's graphic is representative of three of the forms that Worthington and Carruthers (2005) have identified. Firstly, it is a *dynamic* form. It is *full of life and suggestive of action* (Worthington and Carruthers, 2005, p14). Her 'scribble' represents three of the seagulls hiding (it is possible to make out three circles behind the scribbles that were drawn first). Secondly, Amelie has used *iconic* representation. She uses circles to represent all the seagulls and demonstrates through this that she has utilised Gelman and Gallistel's (1978) one-to-one principle. Thirdly, it is *pictographic*. Although not related to the seagull activity, Amelie became taken with a cat in the book. She represents the cat and carefully counts its whiskers, *two on that side and two on that side, is that right? Oh no, there are three there and two there*.

Read more about Carruthers and Worthington's work in Chapter 1.

Carruthers and Worthington (2005) challenge the category given by Hughes (see Chapter 1 for more detail) entitled *idiosyncratic*. They believe that because it appears Hughes did not ask children for an explanation of their work, and he was unable to decode it, he dismissed it. They believe that children make marks only with meaning and that it is the responsibility of the teacher or Early Years practitioner to elicit children's mathematical thinking from discussing their marks with them. The work provided here by Amelie would concur. The apparent scribbling on the right of the page is the seagulls 'hiding'. Indeed, *perception, communication and invention are significant features of their (children's) mathematical graphics. Such a perspective supports a view of children as powerful and creative learners ...* (Worthington and Carruthers, 2005, p6).

2. Deriving facts

Being able to derive facts is an important step in children developing confidence in manipulating numbers and calculating. In its evaluation of the National Numeracy Strategy's second year, Ofsted explicitly mentioned an example in a Reception class where the children were deriving number pairs of bonds to eight through other tasks undertaken (Ofsted, 2001). The QCA (1999) makes explicit mention of the need for children to derive facts, and lists for teachers the expectations for children at each year group.

CASE STUDY: I KNOW 6 AND 4 MAKES 10 FROM THE OTHER WAY YOU CAN MAKE 10 (YEAR 1)

Context
In this case study, Nick has planned to use sticks of ten Multilinks cubes to revisit number bonds to 10.

Curriculum Content
National Curriculum Key Stage 1
Pupils should be taught to:

Ma2.3c: develop rapid recall of number facts: know addition and subtraction facts to 10 and use these to derive facts with totals of 20...

Primary Framework Year 1
Derive and recall all pairs of numbers with a total of 10...

Task
While you are reading this case study, think about how Nick responded to Serena's explanation, building on it by changing his approach with the children.

Nick:	How can we add six and four?
Serena:	(*Immediately, shouting out.*) Six and four make ten!
Nick:	That was very quick, Serena. How did you know that answer so quickly?
Serena:	That is easy. Six and four are ten.
Nick:	OK, can you please explain to us how you know that?
Serena:	Well, I know it from the other way you can make ten.
Nick:	Pardon?
Serena:	From the other way you can make ten. Five and five.
Nick:	Can you explain that again to us, please?
Serena:	(*Sighs.*) Well, five and five is ten (*shows two hands*) and that is the other way you can make ten. So six (*shows six fingers*) and four (*shows four fingers*) are ten too.
Nick:	Thank you, Serena. Let's explore how we can use our fingers to explore other ways of making ten.

Extending subject knowledge

Developing models to derive facts

Nick has used two different types of models in this case study. He had planned to show Multilink sticks of ten, which he had prepared for the lesson. By breaking the stick and hiding part of it, the children were able to visualise how many cubes were missing and practise their number bonds to ten. Spontaneously, however, one of the children demonstrated a number fact using her fingers. At this point, Nick decided to encourage all the children to use their fingers to make other number bonds before returning to the sticks.

Physical use of models is a stepping stone for children to be able to develop their own mental models (Hansen, 2007). Models are powerful tools for all people to carry out mathematical tasks (Lesh and English, 2005; English and Watters, 2005; Lesh and Zawojewski, 2007), but it is necessary to encourage children to move on from their existing strategies (e.g. using fingers to count up) when a more effective method could be carried out mentally (Thompson, 1999).

3. The multiplication facts

Knowing the multiplication facts by heart is important knowledge for children to have gained by the end of their primary schooling. This is because multiplication facts exist in so many aspects of mathematics and are used within them often. More specifically for children, they are multiplying (dividing, adding and subtracting!) on a daily basis in a range of everyday tasks and to be able to recall the answers efficiently supports their many roles in life.

Read more about using multiplication facts in calculations in Chapter 4.

CASE STUDY: PATTERNS IN THE MULTIPLICATION FACTS (YEAR 4)

Context

In this case study, Gill has taught her class to use the calculator to generate the multiples of any given times table very quickly. She asks them to choose their own times table and to discuss the patterns that they see in the multiples with their partner. Two children are discussing their pattern and become excited by the digital root of the multiples of nine.

Curriculum Content

National Curriculum Key Stage 2

Pupils should be taught to:

Ma2.2b: recognise and describe number patterns, including two- and three-digit multiples of 2, 5 or 10, recognising their patterns and using these to make predictions; make general statements.

Primary Framework Year 4

Derive and recall multiplication facts up to 10 x 10, the corresponding division facts and multiples of numbers to 10 up to the tenth multiple.

Task

Explore the digital roots of multiples other than nine. What are the digital roots of the multiples of three? What about the digital roots of prime numbers (with the exception of 3)?

Ashleigh:	I've filled up the paper.
Ben:	Yeah. What patterns are there?
Ashleigh:	It is the nine times table.
Ben:	Hmmmm. 9, 18, 27, 36, 45, 54 – hey! When you go down the units, it goes 9, 8, 7, 6, 5, 4, 3, 2, 1, 0 and then it starts from 9 again!
Ashleigh:	Oh yeah, that's cool! And the tens digits go up – 1, 2, 3, 4, 5, 6, 7, 8, 9 oh, 9 again. It doesn't quite work.
Ben:	What happens if you add the digits together for each one?
Ashleigh:	Huh?
Ben:	Well, 9 is 9 but then 1 and 8 is 9, and 2 and 7 is 9, and 3 and 6 is 9 –
Ashleigh:	Yeah! And 4 and 5 is 9! But what about 99? That doesn't work.
Ben:	It does, 'cos 9 add 9 is 18, and 1 add 8 is 9! Cool!
Ashleigh:	That is so good! Does it work for all of them, then?
Ben:	I don't know. Try 562 × 9.
Ashleigh:	That won't work!
Ben:	That is 5,058.
Ashleigh:	See!
Ben:	No, 5 add 0 add 5 add 8 … that is 18 and then that makes 9 too!
Gill:	What have you two found out?
Ben:	We've found out loads about the nine times table.
Ashleigh:	Yeah, all the digits make 9 when you add them together.
Gill:	Great! You have been calculating the digital root of the multiples of nine.

> 9
> 18
> 27
> 36
> 45
> 54
> 63
> 72
> 81
> 90
> 99
> 108
> 117
> 126
> 135

Extending subject knowledge

Patterns in the multiplication facts

REMINDER

A pattern, regardless of it being a number pattern, linear pattern made of colours or a tessellating pattern, goes on infinitely.

Children learn the multiplication facts in a range of ways. Some may picture a pattern of multiples coloured in on a 100-square, or perhaps visualising jumps on a number line may be useful. Others may recall a certain rhythm to help them learn some facts (such as 'six eights are forty-eight'). Others may rely on doubling (and doubling again and again!) to quickly calculate the answers to many tables. Other children may learn a song (e.g. 'Three is a magic number' by Embrace) to remember a times table. Some will revel in competition-based games to learn their tables. Remember most children will employ a range of strategies to recall different number facts, as not all children learn the same way all the time.

Using the multiples listed in a column is another way to encourage children to explore particular patterns in times tables. They may be able to answer questions such as why does this times table never end in a four? Or why does that times table always have a digital root of 3, 6 or 9?

Using your own subject knowledge to develop the children's understanding of multiplication facts

All of the examples above use various strategies for children to familiarise themselves further with the multiplication facts and therefore develop a deeper understanding and quicker recall of the answers.

Another class-wide technique to encourage children to learn multiplication tables is to have a 'table of the week'. Have a number of cards displayed around the room with the fact on (say, $6 \times 7 = 42$) and refer to it as often as you can during the week. At appropriate times during the week, take time to go through all the past tables of the week to check children's recall. (This is also a good suggestion to give to parents who want to help their children learn facts at home – by getting children to write out their own facts to stick in prominent places around the house, the practice has already begun!)

One way to make the link between the multiplication facts and the division facts is to talk to children about 'families of facts'. So when you are displaying your 'table of the week', ask the children in different ways to help support this link. For example, 'six sevens are (all together) forty-two', 'what is six multiplied by seven?', 'so what is seven times six?', 'forty-two divided by six equals?' and so on.

It is useful to develop your own knowledge of the multiplication facts during your mathematics teaching in school. When you are using them on a daily basis with your class, your skills in rapid recall will develop at a surprising rate.

4. Rounding

There are several purposes for rounding numbers. These are often overlooked when we teach (or are taught) to 'round to the nearest whole number' or 'round to five significant digits'. If we encourage children to round numbers within a context, they will begin to manipulate numbers effectively during mental calculation in order to estimate an answer, round numbers to make them more manageable, understand our place value system better, and undertake more effective mental calculations. Heirdsfield and Cooper (2004) demonstrated that poor estimators lacked 'number sense' and used rounding as the only strategy for calculating results. Rounding numbers appropriately was very important, and people with a higher level of 'number sense' were able to do this effectively.

You can read more about estimation, which is closely related to rounding, in Chapter 6.

CASE STUDY: A TRIP TO THE FOOTBALL GROUND (YEAR 4)

Context

In this case study, Alan takes his Year 4 class to the neighbouring football ground. He utilises the links that the club has with the school (the club practises on some of the school's grounds) and he takes advantage of the fact that the majority of the class are avid football supporters. He uses this opportunity to introduce the notion of rounding to the children and plans to use rounding in the mathematics lessons later in the week to help them check answers to their addition and subtraction calculations.

Curriculum Content

National Curriculum Key Stage 2
Pupils should be taught to:
Ma2.1e: make mental estimates of the answers to calculations; check results.

Primary Framework Year 4
Use knowledge and understanding of rounding, number operations and inverses to estimate and check calculations.

Task

While you are reading this case study, think about how introducing the children to rounding in this context will support them in their mental calculations and check the accuracy of results as they progress through school mathematics.

Alan:	So here we are right in the middle of Christchurch Park. Can anyone estimate, or does anyone know, the seating capacity of the ground?

(Estimations are given from several of the children, ranging from four thousand to fifteen thousand.)

Alan:	OK, there is quite a range of suggestions there. The Main Stand there holds 1,200 people. Does that help you at all?

(Further discussion occurs, where the children consider how many people may be able to sit and/or stand in the various stands of the ground. They then add those up to come to an estimate of six thousand.)

Alan:	Well, you have decided upon a good estimation there everyone, because on the club's official website, it states that the Park holds approximately 6,400 supporters.
Children:	*(General cheers and some discussion in pairs.)*
Alan:	How often do you think the ground is full to capacity?
James:	Not often. I went on Boxing Day with Dad and Uncle Don and there were nearly three and a half thousand there. It was pretty full. But usually when I go it isn't that busy. I reckon you'd only get it that full if it was an FA cup final . . . or when they played off for the league.
Alan:	That is very interesting, James. Do you know exactly how many people were at that game on Boxing Day?
James:	No, but my uncle said that it was nearly three and a half thousand.
Alan:	Your uncle is right. I have the list of fixtures and results here from the team and it says that there were 3,419 people in attendance. Why do you all think that James' Uncle Don said that there were nearly three and a half thousand people here, rather than 3,419 people?
Fern:	It is easier to say three and a half than it is to say three thousand, four hundred and whatever.
Hayley:	And it is easier to remember the easy number.
Alan:	Those are good suggestions. Is it important for us to know *exactly* how many people attended the game?
Children:	No.

Alan:	No, because knowing that there were nearly three and a half thousand people here tells us that it was just over half of the capacity of the ground. (*Pause.*) But who would need to know exactly how many people attended?
Sarah:	The football club.
Alan:	Why?
Sarah:	Well, they need to know how many tickets they sold and how many people are supporting the team.
David:	The people who have the hotdog and burger vans need to know, 'cos then they know how many things to sell.
Alan:	Yes, well done. So, sometimes knowing a number exactly is important, but then at other times, knowing the approximate number is useful enough.

The following day, Alan presented the table below to the children and asked them to work in pairs to complete the final column. He encouraged them to use phrases such as nearly, just under/over, a quarter/half/three-quarters/ third. Their ideas were discussed in the plenary of the lesson and Alan introduced the term 'rounding' to them. He also set them homework to think about where else they might use rounding in their everyday experiences.

Home games to date this season:

DATE	COMPETITION	ATTENDANCE	Uncle Don might say ...
14/07	Friendly	1,248	
17/07	Friendly	1,469	
21/07	Friendly	740	
11/08	League Two	3,633	
25/08	League Two	2,980	
29/09	League Two	2,688	
12/10	League Two	4,761	
15/10	Lancs Cup	594	
10/11	FA Cup	2,730	
26/12	League Two	3,419	
29/12	League Two	2,371	

Extending subject knowledge

Using context to formally introduce a new mathematical idea to pupils

Alan used the football ground context to good effect with his class in this case study. First, he tapped into the notion of 'purpose' (this is discussed in some detail in Chapter 2) to engage the children's interest in rounding. Most of the children had attended games at Christchurch Park and so they were building on existing experiences. Second, Alan had prepared the lesson well, He knew exactly what his learning objectives were and had brought with him the attendances of the games that season. Third, as soon as James had mentioned a rounded figure in the class discussion, Alan was able to use that as a key focus for the discussion. Fourth, Alan attempted to encourage the pupils to think about when rounded numbers can be used and when we have to be more specific.

You can read more about estimation, which is closely related to rounding, in Chapter 6.

Using your own subject knowledge to develop the children's understanding of rounding

There are many other contexts that you could use to develop children's under-standing of rounding. For example, the Mars Polar Lander that crashed in December 1999 on Mars could have landed in a crater (see, for example, BBC News, 2000). A NASA scientist needs to be more specific in their measurements than someone measuring up for a new double-glazed window! These types of scenarios could be discussed with Upper Key Stage 2 children.

In the case study, although Alan used real figures from the football club's website, he carefully selected the fixtures that were most helpful for the children to begin to explore the rounding that he wanted them to. He used numbers such as 1,248 to try and encourage the children to think of this as 'nearly one and a quarter thousand', to help them develop their flexible understanding of numbers and their under-standing of the place value system.

5. Factors and divisibility rules

Being able to use factors and the divisibility rules aids children in their mental calcula-tions and also in their ability to check the accuracy of their written calculations.

For example, knowing the factors of 18 allows us to calculate the answer to 12×18 mentally. If we know that two of the factors of 18 are 2 and 9 (and therefore 2, 3 and 3) then we can calculate $12 \times 2 \times 2 \times 3$ to work out the answer. (I'd calculate $18 \times 3 = 54$, then double and double again.)

Table 3.1 The divisibility rules

The number is divisible by …	if …
2	the last digit is even
3	the sum of the digits is divisible by 3
4	the number made by the last two digits is divisible by 4
5	the last digit is 0 or 5
6	the number is divisible by 2 *and* 3 (because $2 \times 3 = 6$!)
8	the last three digits are divisible by 8
9	the sum of the digits is divisible by 9
10	the number ends in a 0
11	add every second digit, then subtract each of the remaining digits from that sum, and the answer is 0 or divisible by 8 (like the 7s, you may have to do more times!)
12	it is divisible by 3 *and* 4 (because $3 \times 4 = 12$)

The divisibility rules (see Table 3.1) can help us to check possible answers and to think about what the possible factors of a number might be. They can also be used to discover patterns about the multiplication tables, such as the use of the digital root in the previous case study to find out more about the nine times table.

CASE STUDY: FACTOR CATERPILLARS (YEAR 5)

Context
In this case study, Emily, the teaching assistant, is working with a class of lower attaining Year 5 pupils to find the factors of numbers. They are creating caterpillars by writing one factor on each segment of the body. They are finding that some caterpillars are very short (e.g. the '7' caterpillar has only two segments: 1 and 7) and others are much longer (e.g. the '24' caterpillar has eight segments: 1, 2, 3, 4, 6, 8, 12 and 24).

Curriculum Content
Underline: *National Curriculum Key Stage 2*
Pupils should be taught to:

Ma2.3h: multiply and divide, at first in the range 1 to 100, then for particular cases of larger numbers by using factors, distribution or other methods.

Underline: *Primary Framework Year 5*
Identify pairs of factors of two-digit whole numbers and find common multiples.

Task
While you are reading this case study, think about how the use of display can develop children's mathematical understanding. Also consider how recording mathematics in different formats can support some children to record their work in a more effective way.

The lower attainment pupils are working on creating factor caterpillars for their multiple garden display that they began yesterday with Emily, the teaching assistant. The multiple garden consists of flowers made from a number of their choice in the centre of a paper cup cake from which petals of the multiples of that number protrude. For example:

Their task in today's lesson is to create a number of factor caterpillars for the garden and compare their lengths. For example:

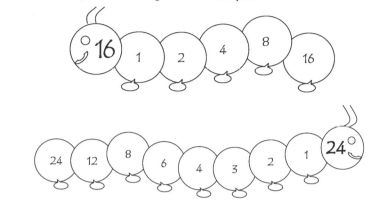

Extending subject knowledge

Finding common factors and multiples

The two lessons above were part of a wider unit on using factors and multiples to find the properties of prime numbers, square numbers and rectangular numbers. Throughout the task, and during the plenary, the children discussed how long their caterpillars were. They sorted the caterpillars into groups: those that had only two factors (which they concluded were the **prime** numbers), those that had an *odd* number of factors (which they concluded were the **square** numbers, e.g. 16 has three factors: 1, 4, 16) and those that had an *even* number of factors (which they concluded were the remaining numbers: the **rectangular** numbers).

You can read about how to use factors to make mental calculation easier in Chapter 4.

Under the guidance of their teaching assistant and teacher, all the pupils in the class were able to use the group's display to look at the numbers that had '2' as a factor and conclude they were all even numbers (and therefore to generalise that all even numbers have 2 as one of their factors).

They also looked at common multiples in the flowers. For example, having seen that 6 was a multiple common to the '2' flower and the '3' flower they noted that it was interesting that $2 \times 3 = 6$. Using this observation, they then looked for other common multiples, using a Venn diagram to classify the multiples:

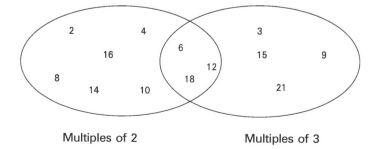

Multiples of 2   Multiples of 3

6. Multiplying and dividing by multiples of ten

There are a large number of teaching resources available that tell us when multiplying 85 by 100, *place two zeros after 85* (Schlessinger Media, 2004) or to *just move the decimal point one place to the right for each factor of ten* (Fisher, 2004). However, the former is misleading because if we are multiplying 8.5 by 100 and place two zeros at the end, the outcome is 8.500, which is incorrect. The latter, while perhaps avoiding an incorrect outcome, does not explain with any meaning and reference to place value why this procedure works.

Read more about the place value system in Chapter 2.

CASE STUDY: THE DIGITS MOVE, NOT THE DECIMAL POINT (YEAR 6)

Context
In this case study, Lorraine is encouraging her Year 6 pupils to look at the effect of multiplication and division by powers of 10 (10, 100, 1000 and so on) on the value of the digits in numbers. She has set up six chairs at the front of the class. They represent the thousands, hundreds, tens, units/ones (then, at a table, a decimal point), tenths and hundredths.

Curriculum Content
<u>National Curriculum Key Stage 2</u>
Pupils should be taught to:

Ma2.1a: make connections in mathematics and appreciate the need to use numerical skills and knowledge when solving problems in other parts of the mathematics curriculum

Ma2.2c: multiply and divide decimals by 10 or 100

<u>Primary Framework Year 6</u>
Use knowledge of place value . . . to derive related multiplication and division facts involving decimals.

Task
While you are reading this case study, think about which effects of multiplying and dividing by powers of 10 the task helps children to understand.

| Mary | Gail | Imran | Sean |

Lorraine:	Can we please read out the number that is being shown here?
All:	Thirty-six point seven.
Lorraine:	Good. Mary, you are the digit 3. What number are you representing?
Mary:	Thirty.
Lorraine:	Yes. And Gail? What digit are you?
Gail:	Six.

Lorraine:	Good. What number are you?
Gail:	Six.
Lorraine:	Yes! How many ones are you representing?
Gail:	Six!
Lorraine:	Yes! Haha! Wasn't that easy! Sean, you are the digit seven. But what fraction of a unit are you presenting?
Sean:	Tenths.
Lorraine:	Good. So, how many tenths are you?
Sean:	Seven tenths.
Lorraine:	How would we say that as a decimal number?
Sean:	Point seven.
Lorraine:	Yes. Micha, I'd like you to show us what happens if we multiply 36.7 by 10.
Micha:	(*She takes a card with 0 on it and sits on Sean's chair. Sean moves to Gail's chair, and so on.*)

Mary	Gail	Sean	Imran	Micha

Lorraine:	What number have we created now, class?
All:	Three hundred and sixty seven.
Lorraine:	Tell me what you did, Micha?
Micha:	Well, I knew that 36.7 times 10 was 367.
Lorraine:	How did you know that?
Micha:	Hmmm . . . I'm not sure . . . well, if you multiply something by 10, it makes it ten times bigger.
Lorraine:	Yes, that is a great way of thinking about it, Micha. Let's check that out. Mary, what number were you before?
Mary:	30.
Lorraine:	And what number are you now?
Mary:	300.
Lorraine:	Good. And is 300 ten times bigger than 30?
All:	Yes.
Lorraine:	Gail? You were six and now you are ...?
Gail:	60.
Lorraine:	Yes. Ten times bigger than 6 is 60. And Sean?
Sean:	I was point seven and now I am 7. Seven is ten times point seven.
Lorraine:	Well done! When we multiplied our number by 10, we made it ten times bigger and the digits moved one place to the left. So what if we were to multiply this number by 10?

The discussion continued to generalise movement to the left and right when multiplying and dividing by ten, hundred, thousand. Lorraine also used the whiteboard to record how the digits moved between the places.

Extending subject knowledge

Using resources and discussion to reinforce multiplication and division of powers of ten

Lorraine had thought carefully about how she wanted to reinforce the effect of multiplication and division on the value of the digits in numbers when she was working with her pupils. By placing the pupil holding the decimal point behind a table, they were unable to move and so the digits had to move to their appropriate places according to the multiplication or division being undertaken. Lorraine reinforced for the pupils the value of the digits in their places before and after undertaking the calculations.

Lorraine followed this up in a PE lesson by including a warm-up where the children sang the following song, stepping to the left or the right as appropriate. She found later that the children were singing the song during mathematics lessons that required them to calculate answers to these types of calculations.

> **Sung to the tune of 'She'll be Coming Round the Mountain'**
>
> If you multiply by ten you move to the left (*shout and move*) one place!
> If you divide by ten you move to the right (*shout and move*) one place!
> If you multiply or divide by ten, then you move to the left or right,
> You move the digits to the left or the right one place (*shout*) Yee haa!
>
> *Chorus:*
> We're singing that's the way you times or divide by ten (*shout*) or one hundred or one
>   thousand!
> We're singing that's the way you times or divide by ten (*shout*) or one hundred or one
>   thousand!
> You move the digits left one place if you multiply by ten
> And it is to the right you move one place if you divide instead.
>
> If you multiply by one hundred you move to the left (*shout and move*) two places!
> If you divide by one hundred you move to the right (*shout and move*) two places!
> If you multiply or divide by one hundred, then you move to the left or right,
> You move the digits to the left or the right two places (*shout*) Yee haa!
>
> *Chorus*
> If you multiply by one thousand you move to the left (*shout and move*) three places!
> If you divide by one thousand you move to the right (*shout and move*) three places!
> If you multiply or divide by one thousand, then you move to the left or right,
> You move the digits to the left or the right three places (*shout*) Yee haa!
>
> *Chorus*

FURTHER READING
Read Lawton (2005) in A. Hansen (ed.) *Children's errors in mathematics*. Exeter: Learning Matters, for more on children's misconceptions about multiplication and division by powers of ten.

In Chapter 4 you can read more about how children's knowledge of division by fractions helped them notice patterns.

4
Calculating

Introduction

This chapter is the third of three in this book involving number. Number is a substantial part of the mathematics curriculum. There is a plethora of books dedicated to supporting your subject and pedagogic knowledge in number (e.g. Frobisher et al., 1999; Koshy and Murray, 2002; Thompson, 1999). Calculating can be undertaken only with an understanding of number, the ability to count, and knowing and using number facts which were covered in Chapters 2 and 3.

In this chapter we will look at five aspects of calculating.

1. *Using the inverse operation to solve a problem*. How can teachers introduce the concept of the inverse operation? What are connectionist teachers? This section includes a case study involving Year 1 children using 'counting on' as a strategy to solve difference or subtraction problems.

2. *Mental calculation facts*. What skills are required to calculate mentally? How can clear progression be used to support a mixed-attainment class? How can I develop my subject knowledge through designing tasks? This case study shows how a student teacher prepares to teach a mixed-attainment Key Stage 2 class halving and doubling.

3. *Written methods*. When should written methods be introduced to children? How should they be introduced? How can children undertake calculations with understanding? What written methods should be used? This includes a Year 4 case study about a child with English as an Additional Language who introduces a new subtraction method to the teacher and the class.

4. *Calculating with fractions and decimals*. Why does dividing by a fraction make the answer bigger? How can number patterns be used to develop children's understanding of multiplying and dividing by fractions and decimals? This includes two case studies. The first is with a Year 4 class who use capacity to explore dividing by one quarter. The second is with a Year 6 case study who explore patterns to generalise rules about multiplying and dividing by decimals.

5. *The calculator*. What are the National Curriculum requirements? How do these differ from the guidance of the PNS Framework for mathematics? How can calculators develop children's mathematical thinking? How do 'real-life' situations develop children's mathematical thinking? The case study looks at a group of Year 6 pupils who use calculators to support their problem-solving.

1. Using the inverse operation to solve a problem

It is often an intuitive or automatic response by student teachers I work with to encourage children to turn a subtraction question (e.g. $23 - 7 = \square$) into an addition in order to find the solution. However, this would require the children to calculate the answer to A: $7 + \square = 23$, which they find very difficult, or B: $\square + 7 = 23$, which they find even more difficult (Foster, 1997).

Fusion (1986) and Fusion and Willis (1988) suggested that teaching counting on (option A above) as a strategy for solving subtraction problems may be a useful method for young children because they are good at counting on. At the time, Fusion's work was specifically related to subtraction from numbers no greater than 18 (with 9 being the greatest number being subtracted). Fusion's next step was to introduce column subtraction for numbers greater than 18 and teach decomposition.

Trials demonstrated that her counting on method gained correct answers, but in our current climate, column algorithms are not introduced until much later in the curriculum. Additionally, Thompson (1999) warns that how we use 'counting on' to solve 'take away' problems is not an intuitive method that children use. Fusion (1986) pre-empts this argument, by explaining that teachers should not read $9 - 4$ as 'nine take away four' but as 'nine subtract four', thus teaching the children to find the difference between these numbers by counting up from 4 to 9.

This has resonance with current calculation methods for subtraction, as the use of the empty number line is encouraged from around Year 2 as a resource for children to calculate subtraction questions by finding the difference.

CASE STUDY: COUNTING ON TO FIND THE DIFFERENCE (YEAR 1)

Context
In this case study, Elaine is working with her class to encourage them to think about 'how many more' counters are needed to put in the jar to make the target number. She supports their counting and mental work with writing the number sentences and using a number track on the whiteboard.

Curriculum Content
National Curriculum Key Stage 1
Pupils should be taught to:

Ma2.3a: understand subtraction as both 'take away' and 'difference' and use the related vocabulary; recognise that subtraction is the inverse of addition; give the subtraction corresponding to an addition and vice versa; use the symbol '=' to represent equality; solve simple missing number problems.

Primary Framework Year 1
Understand subtraction as 'take away' and find a 'difference' by counting up

Task
How does Elaine use a range of resources to support the children's mathematical thinking?

Elaine:	I have brought into school one of my favourite containers.
Flo:	It is blue!
Elaine:	It is blue and blue is one of my favourite colours, but there is something else about this container that I think makes it special. Can you see what is special about it?
Imran:	It has a ten on it.
Elaine:	Yes, Imran! It has the number ten on it. Can you guess why I really like the number ten?
Imran:	It has a one and a zero in it.
Elaine:	You are right, it does. Let's all draw large number tens in the air. Altogether, now: The number one, from the top in a line down to the bottom. Then, the zero, from the top and around, back up to the top. Well done everybody. Where else do we see this number written?
Neville:	On my door.
Elaine:	Well done, Neville. You live at number ten High Street, don't you?
Usma:	My sister is ten.
Elaine:	Is she? That's interesting, Usma. There are more reasons why I like the number ten. How many toes do we have?
All:	Ten!
Elaine:	And fingers? (*Shows fingers.*)
All:	Ten.
Elaine:	Good. It also helps me with my counting to ten. Would you like me to show you how it helps me?
All:	Yes!
Elaine:	I am going to start by putting eight counters into the container. Can you help me count them in to the container?
All:	1, 2, 3, 4, 5, 6, 7, 8
Elaine:	Good. Now, there need to be ten counters in my container, but we have only eight. How many more will I need to make ten?
Ali:	Two.
Elaine:	Let's try two. I have two more counters here (*shows them to the class*). We have eight in here already, so that is nine (*drops the first counter*) and ten (*drops the second counter*). So, let's think about what we did there. We had eight counters in the container (*writes '8' on the board*). And we wanted to know how many more we needed to make ten in the container. (*Writes + ☐ = 10 on the board*) And how many more did we need to put in? (*Points to the ☐.*)
All:	Two.
Elaine:	Let's check. (*She removes the transparent counters and places them on the overhead projector.*) We have the 1, 2, 3, 4, 5, 6, 7, 8 counters that we put in first, and then there were two more to make ten. (*She places these on the OHP.*) 1, 2, 3, 4, 5, 6, 7, 8, 9, 10. Well done, we added two more to make 10. (*Writes a '2' in the box.*) Let's have a look at our number track. We started with eight, and we added two more. Count with me...
All:	9, 10.
Elaine:	Let's try another one. How many should we put in my container this time?

Extending subject knowledge

Making connections to support children's learning

In this case study, Elaine used a *connectionist* (Askew et al., 1997a) approach to her teaching. Askew et al. (1997b) identified a number of links between teachers' approach and their work with children. They found that connectionist teachers:

- view mental calculations as part of using relationships to develop 'mental agility' and flexible mental strategies to calculate;
- believe that all pupils, regardless of their level of attainment, should be challenged mathematically;
- used discussion as a key feature of their lessons to support pupil learning;
- saw mathematical thinking (use and application of mathematics) as a way of developing mathematical knowledge and understanding.

Wherever possible, Elaine used the children's everyday knowledge of mathematics, mathematical symbols and the children's activity (counting into the container) to help them make sense of the activity. For example, she asked the children where they had seen the number ten previously. This supported the lower attaining children to count up to a number that they were familiar with in a range of situations. She used OHP counters to check the answer and reinforce the calculation. Elaine also modelled the number sentences on the board, using numerals and symbols to represent the calculations that the children were undertaking. Later in the lesson, she used the children's fingers to think about counting up to ten and challenge the higher attainers in their recall of number bonds to ten (and then twenty).

Read more about counting on in graphs in Chapter 7.

2. Mental calculation facts

Murray (2003) writes extensively about mental mathematics. In doing so, she defines mental mathematics, identifies its role within numeracy, discusses methods and considers the implications of these aspects for teachers, demonstrating its complexity. Simply put, however, *an ability to calculate mentally lies at the heart of much of mathematics* (DfES, 2001, p135). There are a range of skills required to calculate mentally. These include (DfES, 2001, p136):

- remembering number facts and recalling them without hesitation;
- using known facts to figure out new facts;
- drawing on a repertoire of mental strategies to work out calculations, with some thinking time;
- understanding and using the relationships between operations to work out answers and check results;
- approximating calculations to judge whether or not an answer is about the right size;
- applying skills to solve numerical problems.

> **FURTHER READING**
> The PNS (2006) guidance paper on oral and mental work identifies six features that can help support teachers in developing a purpose to oral and mental work in mathematics.

CASE STUDY: USING HALVING AND DOUBLING FROM YEAR 1 TO 6

Context

In this case study, Eamonn is discussing with his student teacher, Sonia, how she might organise a lesson with his KS2 class, where the pupils' NC levels of attainment range from Level 1 to Level 5. He wants her to revisit halving and doubling numbers with all the children.

Curriculum Content

<u>National Curriculum Key Stage 1</u>
Pupils should be taught to:

Ma2.2b: recognise the relationship between halving and doubling.

<u>National Curriculum Key Stage 2</u>
Pupils should be taught to:

Ma2.3g: halve and double any two-digit number.

<u>Primary Framework</u>
Year 1: Solve practical problems that involve combining groups of 2, 5 or 10.
Year 2: Use practical informal methods and related vocabulary to support multiplication and division.
Year 3: Find unit fractions of numbers and quantities.
Year 4: Find fractions of numbers, quantities or shapes.
Year 5: Find fractions using division.
Year 6: Relate fractions to multiplication and division.

Task

What other ways might the children explore halving and doubling when they are in a class with such a spread of attainment?

Sonia: I'm really struggling as to how I might teach the whole class about halving and doubling when there is such a spread of attainment.

Eamonn: I understand. Let's start by thinking why we want the children to be able to halve and double numbers.

Sonia: Well, sometimes doubling a number can be an easy way of working out an answer. Like you can double and double again to work out what four times a number is.

Eamonn: That's good. If you can talk about that with them, then that will be really helpful to them, to see why they might want to practise their doubling. They might be able to come up with some other reasons to, because we talked about using 'near doubles' to derive answers to calculations last term. I also talked with the Year 6 children about how historically only halving and doubling was used to calculate.

Sonia: OK. But how do I get them to practise their doubling and halving all together? Keiran is working at Level 1 and then Jessica is easily at Level 5.

Eamonn: As you know, I don't always teach the whole class together at the same time, especially when I am introducing a new topic or idea to them. But, because they are all confident with halving and doubling, one way to approach it might be to provide each group of children with a set of question cards aimed at challenging them appropriately.

Sonia: So how would I manage that? They would all have different answers and I'm not sure how I'd keep them all together.

Eamonn: Any possible ideas, though?

Sonia: Well, I guess that I could ask them to turn one card at a time over – that way there would only be five answers at a time.

REMINDER
Grouping children by level of attainment is only one method of managing pupils' learning. Try a range of grouping strategies, such as self-selected, or mixed attainment.

Eamonn:	Yes, that's a possibility. But, do you really have to remain 'in charge' like that, and require them to answer questions one at a time? They are good at working independently.
Sonia:	No, I guess not. (*Pause.*) They could play snap – or even a game of 'memory', because I could get them to work in groups of three or four. The questions could be on one card and they have to match it with the answer.
Eamonn:	That's an excellent idea. Or just another way of asking the same question. So reinforcing that four times six can also be six times two times two.
Sonia:	Oh yeah.
Eamonn:	You could use the guidance in this booklet to help you with making up the questions. Remember to focus on National Curriculum levels though, rather than on year group.
Sonia:	Great, thanks very much.

FURTHER READING
Eamonn was referring to QCA (1999) *Teaching mental calculation strategies: guidance for teachers at Key Stages 1 and 2.* London: QCA.

Later, Sonia produced the following sheet to help her create her memory game cards:

Level 1	6+6=12	2+2=4	Double 10 = 20	4 + 4 = 4 x 2	Half of 14 = 7	Double 5 = 10	3 + 3 = 6	8 + 8 = 16
Level 2	6+6 = 6 x 2	Double 8 is 16	Half of 30 is 15	8 x 2 = double 8	Half of 50 is 25	Double 50 is 100	Double 11 = 11+11	70+70 = 140
Level 3	Double 16 is 16+16	Half of 140 is 70	Double 40 is 40 x 2	13 x 5 = 13 x 10 / 2	Half of 700 is 350	Half of 18 = 18 ÷ 2	12 doubled and doubled again is 12 x 4	12 x 20 = 12 X 10 x 2
Level 4	120 x 4 = 120 x 2 x 2	Half of 840 = 420	46 x 4 = 46 X 2 x 2	30% of £24 = 10% of £24 x 3	3.2 ÷ 2 = 1.6	Quarter of 4.8 = 4.8 halved and halved again	25% of 1000 = 50% of 500	0.6 doubled = 1.2
Level 5	6.5 x 4 = 6.5 x 2 x 2	35% of 50 = 10% of 50 x 3½	Half of 4.216 = 4.216 ÷ 2	Quarter of 12.8 = 12.8 ÷ 2 ÷ 2	25 x 248 = (248÷4) x 100	8 x 2.4 = 2.4 doubled three times	1/8th of 12 = 12÷2÷2÷2	VAT = 10% + 5% + 2.5%

Extra game rule: Any child who can calculate the correct answer (if not shown on the card) gets an extra point. Any child can challenge the answer and give the correct one, but if they are wrong, they lose a point! If the answer is already given, the child can state another way of calculating the answer, based on halving and doubling. Same challenge rules apply, but only if answer is incorrect.

Figure 4.1 Planning sheet for the memory game cards

Extending subject knowledge

Identifying appropriate progression

As a student teacher, Sonia was struggling with ideas for teaching a class of children with such an attainment range. Although this particular case study focuses on a Key Stage 2 class, a similar attainment range can be found in a large number of single or mixed classes in many schools so this situation is not unusual. In classrooms where there is a very narrow attainment band, it is equally important to be aware of progression, to ensure that you build on what the children already know and have an appropriately planned learning trajectory for them all.

In this case study, Sonia's challenge was twofold. First, she was required to appropriately challenge all the children. Second, she needed to construct a manageable task (for her and for the children) that enabled this to happen. Through professional dialogue with her mentor, Sonia was able to respond to these and develop her own subject knowledge at the same time.

Developing your own subject knowledge through task design

It is interesting to note that as Sonia created the questions on the cards, the process helped her to develop her own pedagogical subject knowledge in two ways.

- By focusing in detail on the progression from group to group, she was able to explicitly identify examples of numbers that the children would be able to calculate with. This helped her to clarify the types of numbers that were likely to challenge the children in the class and she was able to check the appropriateness of these when the children undertook the task.
- By realising that there was a dual purpose within the content of the cards that she had not intentionally set out to achieve. Her examples enabled the children either to calculate an answer or to consider the relationships between strategies. (For example, adding a number to itself, multiplying a number by two, and doubling a number are all ways to find the answer.) In order to support the children's further development in both of these areas, she set the extra rule for the game which can be seen at the bottom of her sheet.

Finally, Sonia also developed her own mathematical subject knowledge a little as she considered and decided upon the best questions for the pupils working at levels 4 and 5.

3. Written methods

Clarke et al. (2006) reported the findings of a longitudinal study where they followed 323 Australian children from 5 to 12 years of age through their schooling to look at their mental computational strategies. The reason that this study is mentioned here (in a section on written methods) is that, surprisingly, they found a dip in the children's mental strategies in Grades 3 and 4. They suggest that this might be due to major emphasis on *written algorithms and rote memorisation of number facts in Grades 3 and 4 (often to the exclusion of an emphasis on further developing mental strategies) [which] may be premature and inhibit the development of basic and derived strategies in addition and subtraction, and abstraction in multiplication and division* (Clarke, et al., 2006, p335). In their paper, they recommend *a delay in presenting conventional written algorithms to students and rote memorisation, while encouraging the development of their own invented mental and written methods* (p335).

The National Numeracy Strategy's *Primary Framework for literacy and mathematics* (NNS, 1999) in England did delay the introduction of formal written methods. In doing so, it challenged teachers' and parents' existing methods for teaching calculation to children. Based on research findings, the Framework set out a system by which children moved on to more formal, traditional written algorithms only once they were confident in their mental methods of calculation. Even when written methods are introduced (typically with the empty number line) and developed (moving on to partitioning, expanded or grid methods – depending on the operation – and on to column methods), mental calculation methods were paramount to understanding and successful completion of the written methods.

When the 1999 Framework was first introduced, there was little guidance as to how teachers could effectively introduce the range of written strategies on offer. Through my work with teachers and student teachers, I learned that some were trying to introduce two or even three new methods to their children in a week, with a small minority trying to attempt that number in one day! However, since those early days, there has been far more support for teachers. They are being encouraged to use what works best for their own school and pupils and I no longer hear these scenarios. The recent guidance from the PNS (2007a: 6) explains to teachers that *children are entitled to be taught and to acquire secure mental methods of calculation and one efficient written method of calculation for addition*, subtraction, multiplication and division. Many schools are selecting one method that they feel is most appropriate to their pupils and the teachers' preferred teaching methods, and have agreed to use that one method throughout the school rather than developing a range of methods with their children.

CASE STUDY: A SURPRISE SUBTRACTION METHOD (YEAR 4)

Context

In this case study, Micha, a girl relatively new to the school and the UK, has been working on the subtraction questions that have been set for her group. It is only when Kay comes to mark Micha's work that she notices that she has done it differently to the method that was discussed in class.

Curriculum Content

National Curriculum Key Stage 2
Pupils should be taught to:

Ma2.3i: use written methods to add and subtract positive integers less than 1000

Primary Framework Year 4
Refine and use efficient written methods to add and subtract two-digit and three-digit whole numbers and £.p.

Task

How would you respond to Micha's work?

School's preferred methods	Micha's method
567 − 278 =	567 − 278 =

School's preferred methods:

$$\begin{array}{ccccc} 400 & & 150 & & 17 \\ \cancel{500} & + & \cancel{60} & + & \cancel{7} \\ 200 & + & 70 & + & 8 \\ \hline 200 & + & 80 & + & 9 \end{array}$$

Moving on to:

$$\begin{array}{r} {}^{4\ \ 15\ \ 17} \\ \cancel{567} \\ -\ 278 \\ \hline 289 \end{array}$$

Micha's method:

$$\begin{array}{r} 567 \\ -278 \\ -1 \\ -10 \\ 300 \\ \hline 289 \end{array}$$

Extending subject knowledge

Undertaking written calculations with understanding

The school had decided some time ago to teach children subtraction by partitioning and then move their pupils on to the short form when they were confident in their understanding of the value of the digits in the number and the reasons for partitioning 60 + 7 into 50 + 17. The children were encouraged, when moving on to the

REMINDER

c − b = a
minuend (c) −
subtrahend (b) =
difference (a).

short form, to verbalise their thinking as they were working through by using the value of the digits, not just the names of the digits.

At first when faced with Micha's work, Kay was unsure what to do. She could see that Micha had calculated the correct answer for each question, but she couldn't work out the method that she had used. Additionally, Kay was concerned because Micha's method seemed rather difficult, and Kay wasn't sure if she understood it herself! But after some working through, Kay did understand Micha's method. She realised that Micha was partitioning the numbers in the same way as the school's method, but she always wrote the answer to the subtraction she carried out (e.g. 60 − 70), even if this resulted in a negative number (e.g. −10). Finally, she added the numbers together (−1 + −10 + 300) to find the solution.

Kay found herself in a dilemma. She had been taught as a pupil to parrot '60 take 70: you can't do that' and she had heard some of her pupils saying that. Kay thought that it either came from her inadvertently modelling that language at times, or from the pupils making that error through their own experience of undertaking subtractions. After all, to her knowledge, the children had never considered subtraction equations that could provide a negative answer! Kay did not know how to deal with this, as she had assumed nine-year-olds were unable to calculate the answers in this way. Additionally, she thought that she might have reinforced that it was impossible to calculate the answer to those types of questions. Yet, Micha was demonstrating that she could.

After some thought, Kay decided that in the following lesson she would ask Micha, who was a confident and well-liked member of the class, to demonstrate to everyone how she had worked out the answers. Kay decided that, at worst, the pupils would be bemused by this 'strange' method of calculation and, at best, some might understand it and even try it out, developing their understanding of subtracting a larger subtrahend from a smaller minuend. She also thought that it would help Micha to use and reinforce, with Kay's support, some English mathematical terminology.

FURTHER READING

Read Chapter 5 by
Gager (2007), in Drews
and Hansen (eds)
*Using resources to
support
mathematical
thinking*. Exeter:
Learning Matters for
more on supporting EAL
pupils in mathematics.

Kay experienced two further dilemmas. Firstly, she knew the technical terms for the minuend and the subtrahend, but was concerned that the answer was technically referred to as the difference. She had always thought that the 'difference' was always a positive number (e.g. the difference between 2 and 5, or 5 and 2 is 3) and this was challenging her own misconception.

Secondly, Kay was unsure how to support Micha to develop her written method. Kay couldn't see a straightforward way for her to use the method she was comfortable with or shorten it, as was the next step for the pupils using the school method. Additionally, she was concerned that Micha could become 'deskilled' if she stopped thinking about subtraction in that way that she was accustomed to. Finally, Kay assumed that Micha was undertaking her method with understanding, but she thought she would work with her further to assess the depth of that understanding. Kay decided that she would be able to address some of her concerns in the following day's lesson, through Micha sharing her method with the other children. She thought that she would also share her new findings with the pupils, that a 'difference' could be a negative number, and use this to challenge some of their misconceptions about 'you can't take y from x'.

4. Calculating with fractions and decimals: why dividing by a fraction makes the answer bigger

In the two case studies that follow, the children are exploring why dividing by a fraction produces a larger number. This challenges the misconception that the children have developed through their experience, where they believe that multiplication always produces a larger number and division always produces a smaller number.

CASE STUDY: THE SUMMER FETE (YEAR 4)

Context
It is June and the Year 4 class have been tasked with organising the drinks stall at the summer fête. They have already spent time in other maths and science lessons looking at the best value cordial and the nutritional information, and they have been carrying out tests around the school to identify the most popular brands and flavours. In this lesson, they are working out how many cups, and therefore number of cordial bottles, they should buy. Their teacher, Siobhan, has been using this opportunity to demonstrate another way to represent quartering, and to introduce the children to dividing by one quarter.

FURTHER READING
Read Chapter 2 by Lawton in Hansen (ed.) (2005) *Children's errors in mathematics*. Exeter: Learning Matters for more on children's misconceptions.

Curriculum Content
<u>National Curriculum Key Stage 2</u>
Pupils should be taught to:

Ma2.4a: choose, use and combine any of the four number operations to solve word problems involving numbers in 'real life', money or measures of length, mass, capacity or time, then perimeter and area.

<u>Primary Framework Year 4</u>
Multiply and divide numbers to 1,000 by 10 and then 100, understanding the effect; relate to scaling up or down.

Task
Think about the value of giving children a task to do that is going to be carried out in reality, such as the summer fete. What advantages does such an authentic task bring to the children's learning?

Siobhan: So, we now know that this bottle that we will mix the cordial in will hold 5 litres of drink. Remind me. How many millilitres would that be?

Jeremy: 5,000.

Siobhan: Well done, Jeremy. 1,000 millilitres is equal to one litre, so in five litres there must be 5,000 millilitres. (*Writes 5l = 5,000ml on the board*.) How many millilitres did we decide were in each drink?

Kate: 250 ml.

Siobhan:	250 millilitres, or ml for short. Good. So, how many cups are there in a litre?
Imani:	Four, miss.
Siobhan:	How did you work that out, Imani?
Imani:	Well, 250 is a quarter of 1,000 and there are 1,000ml in a litre, so one cup is a quarter of a litre.
Siobhan:	Good. Did everyone understand that?
Children:	(*A range of responses, some in agreement, others shaking their heads.*)
Siobhan:	OK. Can someone else explain it to us? Perhaps with a drawing?
Tabia:	I can!
Siobhan:	OK, Tabia – come up here and show us.
Tabia:	Well, there are 1,000ml in a litre. And if you halve that, you get two lots of 500ml. That's half a litre. And if you halve those again, you get, um, 250ml, which is quarter of a litre. And there are four of those.

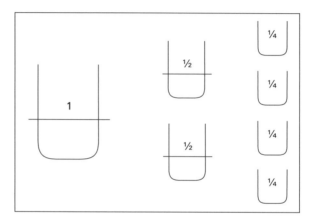

Siobhan:	My word! That is an excellent explanation, Tabia – I really like the way you kept halving the contents of the jugs to get to the answer! So, we have four cups of drink in every litre, but we have five litres in every large bottle. How many cups are there in five litres?
Ewan:	Twenty.
Siobhan:	Yes. So we had 5 litres of cordial (*writes '5' on the board*) and we divided that by ¼ litre drinks *(writes '÷ ¼' on the board)* and that gave us 20 drinks (*writes '= 20' on the board*). Does that make sense?
All:	Yes.
Siobhan:	Hmmmm, I'm not convinced yet. Let's try it out this time. (*She brings out a two-litre bottle filled with water, and a pack of cups.*)
All:	(*General excitement.*)
Siobhan:	OK, everyone. In the last problem, we had five litres that we needed to share between ¼ litre cups. This time there are only two litres (*writes '2 ÷ ¼' on the board*). Shall we try it out this time? Fran, you have been sitting nicely, would you like to come

	up and pour our drinks?
Fran:	Yes. (*Pours each cup, with Siobhan checking on the amount of liquid being poured in to each one.*)
Siobhan:	Well done, Fran. How many cups of cordial do we now have?
All:	Eight.
Siobhan:	(*Completes the number sentence on the board: '2 ÷ ¼ = 8'.*) Hmmm ... I'm wondering if anyone can begin to see a pattern here. If we had one litre of cordial, we'd get four cups. Two litres would make us eight cups ... (*she writes the following on the board, with support from the children*):

$1 \div \frac{1}{4} = 4$

$2 \div \frac{1}{4} = 8$

$3 \div \frac{1}{4} = 12$

$4 \div \frac{1}{4} = 16$

$5 \div \frac{1}{4} = 20$

$6 \div \frac{1}{4} = 24$

$7 \div \frac{1}{4} = 28$

$8 \div \frac{1}{4} = 32$

$9 \div \frac{1}{4} = 36$

$10 \div \frac{1}{4} = 40$

(*The patterns are discussed, the children having identified several. They finally calculate how many litres of cordial they would need to see 300 cups at the fete, and how many bottles of concentrate that would require.*)

CASE STUDY: PATTERNS IN NUMBERS (YEAR 6)

Context
In this case study, Steve is working with the whole class during the plenary of the mathematics lesson. He is using the calculator on the interactive whiteboard to work out division questions, to challenge the pupils' misconception that 'when you divide a number, the answer is always smaller'.

Curriculum Content
<u>National Curriculum Key Stage 2</u>
Pupils should be taught to:

Ma2.2b: recognise and describe number patterns, recognising patterns and using these to make predictions; make general statements ...

<u>Primary Framework Year 6</u>
Relate fractions to multiplication and division ...

Task

How does having a good subject knowledge of place value support children's development of mental calculation work for decimals?

Steve: During our group work, some of the people in my group were a bit confused by what they were finding on their calculators when they were using them to work out division problems. For example, they knew that $20 \div 4 = 5$ and actually, they didn't even have to use their calculator for that! But, when they keyed in $20 \div 0.4$, what answer do you think they got? Talk about it in your pairs, and write your agreed solution on your whiteboards. (*Pause.*) Thank you. Harrison and Jake, can you please tell us all what you have written, and why?

Harrison: Well, we have written 0.5.

Steve: Tell us why.

Harrison: Well, we knew that it had to have the same digit in it – five – because they were the same numbers, twenty and point four. So we thought that it would be 0.5.

Steve: Oh, I see. (*Writes '$20 \div 0.4 = 0.5$' on the board.*) What do others think of that?

Lizzy: I don't think that is right, 'cos 0.5 is a half, and 20 divided by 40 gives a half.

Steve: That is interesting. What do you think of that, Harrison and Jake?

Jake: Yeah, I can see how 0.5 is a half, so it's not right, hmmm.

Steve: Let me write that on the board. We know that $20 \div 4 = 5$. We now know that $20 \div 40 = 0.5$. (*Writes latter above the first number sentence.*)

Maddison: I know! It is $20 \div 0.4 = 50$. There is a pattern there! It was 0.5, then 5, so now it is 50.

Steve: OK, so can you tell us the next number sentence in your pattern?

Maddison: $20 \div 0.04 = 500$.

Steve: Good. Who can give us the equation that would go up here? (*Points to the space above $20 \div 40 = 0.5$.*)

Christian: $20 \div 400 = 0.05$

Steve: Well done! OK, let me see how well you are beginning to understand this. Wipe your whiteboards clean. I am going to write an equation on the middle of my board. I'd like you to copy it. Then, as you have been doing for these ones, I'd like you to derive as many equations up and down your whiteboards as you can. Are you ready?

All: Yes.

Steve: OK. The first number sentence is $24 \div 6 = 4$.

Extending subject knowledge

Using number patterns to support children's understanding of dividing by fractions and decimals

Dividing by fractions is potentially a difficult area to introduce to children. However, both of the teachers in these case studies used patterns and systematic problem-solving and it was evident that the topics were effectively introduced by the teachers and developed by the children in a meaningful context.

Fractions

When dividing by fractions, adults often remember the procedure they were taught in order to calculate the answer. It goes something like, 'turn the fraction upside down and multiply'. That would have worked with the cordial task in the Year 4 case study. The children could have turned the ¼ 'upside down' (to give four divided by one, which is four) and then multiply by four. In fact some of the children alluded to this in the discussions afterwards, noting that 'the pattern goes up in the multiples of four, and isn't that funny, 'cos it is quarters, which are about fours too!' But making a meaningful link as this child did later in the lesson is far more helpful to their mathematical understanding than trying to remember a rule to follow at a later date.

Read more about the meanings of fractions in Chapter 2.

Additionally, it is essential to remember that a fraction is a number in its own right. Therefore, introducing one half as 'one over two' – as if it is actually made up of two whole numbers – is particularly unhelpful to children. As has been demonstrated in the case study above, children are confident manipulating fractions as numbers in their own right. The teacher spoke like this:

Five litres shared into quarter litres gives us twenty.

Note the similarities with ...

Fifty litres shared into ten litres gives us five.

The same meaning of a division (equal sharing) is used in both cases.

Decimals

Procedural 'tips' are remembered by adults when decimal numbers are being multiplied or divided ... remember how you were taught to add the number of places after the decimal point and then do certain things according to that number?

The Year 6 children in this case study were not being taught a rote method such as this without meaning. They were being encouraged to use their place value knowledge to derive facts from known facts. Some of the more able children towards the end of the investigation were beginning to make generalisations and develop their own 'rules' – this is effective, because they are designing their rules with understanding and will be able to use them again more meaningfully.

> REMINDER
> Dividend ÷ divisor = quotient

Additionally, some of the children made the link between the number of decimal places and the size of the answer. They were able to see that making the divisor ten times bigger made the quotient ten times bigger (when the dividend was a whole number).

5. The calculator

The National Curriculum (DfEE, 1999) requires that children in Key Stage 2 are confident and competent users of calculators. This requirement is reflected in Mathematics Test B (Calculator Paper) of the current End of Key Stage 2 National Curriculum Assessment (QCA, 2007). In a departure from the National Curriculum, the PNS (2007b) guidance paper on the use of calculators in the teaching and learning of mathematics provides examples for teachers of Foundation Stage through to Year 6. The guidance paper warns, however, that the teacher should control *the children's access to and use of the calculator* (PNS, 2007b, p4). This could counter the National Curriculum Programme of Study for Using and Applying Mathematics where children are required to *select and use appropriate mathematical equipment, including ICT* (Ma2. 1c).

There is a range of literature (Cole and Newson, 1996; Hembree and Dessart, 1992; Ruthven, 1998) that demonstrates that judicial use of calculators can develop children's mathematical knowledge and understanding through developing their mental calculation strategies, attitude and motivation towards mathematics. Indeed, some studies (Groves and Stacey, 1996; Scheuneman et al., 2002; The Calculator Aware Number Project) have demonstrated that children who use calculators over an extended period of time outperform their counterparts who have had less calculator experience in terms of their computational and estimation skills, and their understanding of number.

CASE STUDY: USING THE MEMORY BUTTON (YEAR 6)

Context
In this case study, Toni is working with her Year 6 class on an investigation about the total monetary value of the items that were given by the 'true love' in the Twelve Days of Christmas. This coincides with some work they have been doing in RE that looks at the Christian symbolism in the song. The children have already been on the Internet and phoned local companies and employers to find the cost of these items (see below). The high attainment group are discussing their findings with Toni.

Curriculum Content
National Curriculum Key Stage 2
Pupils should be taught to:

Ma2.3k: use a calculator for calculations involving several digits, including decimals; use a calculator to solve number problems; know how to enter and interpret money calculations and fractions; know how to select the correct key sequence for calculations with more than one operation.

Primary Framework Year 6
Use a calculator to solve problems involving multi-step calculations

Task
What techniques of using and applying have the children used during this activity? How does Toni introduce the functions on the calculator to the children? In what other contexts might children be able to use the memory functions?

Item	How many?	Cost per item	Source	Total cost
A partridge in a pear tree	1 x 12	Partridge = £32.00 Pear Tree = £22.95 Total: £54.95	www.donaldrussell.com www.donaldrussell.com	
2 turtle doves	2 x 11	£8.00	www.birdtrade.co.uk	
3 french hens	3 x 10	£1.50 per chick	Local poultry farm	
4 calling birds	4 x 9	Free		
5 golden rings	5 x 8	£99.99	www.argos.co.uk	
6 geese a-laying	6 x 7	£26.00	Local poultry farm	
7 swans a-swimming	7 x 6	Toy = £10.99 Postage = £2.49	Soft toy from www.ebay.co.uk	
8 maids a-milking	8 x 5	£4.60/hr	www.hmrc.gov.uk/nmw	
9 ladies dancing	9 x 4	£13.50/hr	Local dance teacher	
10 lords a-leaping	10 x 3	£57.60	www.amazon.co.uk	
11 pipers piping	11 x 2	Bagpipe = £3,850.00 Musician = £25.00/hr	www.inveran.com Local music teacher	
12 drummers drumming	12 x 1	Drum = £149.00 Drummer = £25.00/hr	www.drumlanduk.com Local music teacher	

Toni: How are you all getting on?

Helen: We've worked out how much everything is going to cost separately.

Toni: Good. Let's have a look. You got ten lords a-leaping from a book shop?

Fern: (*Laughs*.) Yeah – we couldn't find out how much a lord costs, or even if they would go to the true love's house, but we found this book.

Toni: £57.60 for a book?

Fern: Yeah, it is by Ruth Dudley Edwards and it is a murder mystery, but it is shipped from the United States. It is called *Ten Lords A-leaping*.

Toni: Good one! So, how are you going to work out the total of all your gifts?

Kate: We have worked out how many of each present there is over the twelve days and put that in the second column. So now we are going to put the total cost of each item in the end column –

Yvonne: (*Interrupting*) – and then add them up.

Toni: Hmmmm. You have quite a lot of work to do there.

Yvonne: Yes, it will take some time but that's OK.

Toni: Can you think of anything that you could use to help you to speed up your calculation?

Kate: We could use a calculator.

Helen: We were going to use a calculator anyway! (*All children laugh*.)

Toni: Tell me how you were going to use it.

Yvonne: We were going to use it to do all the times-ing and then all the adding.

Toni: Can I show you how you might be able to use the calculator more powerfully than that, so that you don't have to do it in two steps?

All: Yes.

Read more about order of operations (BODMAS) in Chapter 1.

Toni:	OK. Let me write down what I think you are going to do. Will you add the cost of the pear tree and the partridge and then multiply that sum by 12?
All:	Yes.
Toni:	So that will look like this: (*Writes: (£32.00 + £22.95) × 12.*)
All:	Yes.
Toni:	Do you remember why we put the brackets around the numbers we are adding?
Fern:	We're doing them first.
Toni:	Good. So, then we're calculating the turtle doves, which are two at eight pounds over the eleven days. (*Adds to the first equation: + £8 × 2 × 11.*) That OK so far?
All:	Yes.
Toni:	We'll do one more together, so I can show you how you can use the calculator more effectively. French hens at £1.50 each. That's reasonable! Multiplied by three for ten days. (*Adds to the equation: + £1.50 × 3 × 10*) Right. So why am I doing all of this for you? Well, let's have a closer look at the calculator. What are some of the keys that you haven't used at school before, or perhaps ones you're not sure what they mean?
Yvonne:	The M+, M−, MC and MR buttons are something I haven't used before.
Toni:	OK. We're going to use those today. Any ideas what they might do, or what the symbols mean?
Fern:	The plus and minus is obvious.
Toni:	Yes. The M stands for memory. So you can ask the calculator to remember numbers for you while you undertake other calculations, and then add or deduct those answers to (or from) that number in the memory.
Kate:	Huh?
Toni:	Let me show you. First, check that the memory is clear. Press MC for memory clear. Now, we want to add the pear tree and partridge. 32 + 22.95. Equals. That gives us 54.95. Multiplied by 12 is 659.4. So, we could do what you suggested earlier, Yvonne, and write £659.40 in that column on your table. Alternatively, we could instruct the calculator to remember that number. So we would press M+, because we are adding it to the memory. Remember we cleared the memory first, so there should be 659.4 in there now. Let's check. (*Presses MR.*) Memory Recall. MR. There it is. Notice that there is also a small M in the corner of the display there too, to remind us there is something in there. Now, let's calculate the turtle doves. That's easy, isn't it. We could do that mentally, but let's do eight times 22. That gives us 176. So if we press M+ again it will add 176 to the amount that is already in the memory. Believe me?
All:	Yes
Toni:	Let's check. MR – memory recall. Yes, look 835.4. That is £659.40 plus £176. You have a go now, Kate, with the French hens.

Extending subject knowledge

Setting complex 'real-life' problems to develop children's mathematical understanding

The design of Toni's task appears straightforward. The idea certainly captured the children's interest and all the children had opinions on which particular presents to buy and where to source them. However, Toni had considered a number of potential difficulties that the children might have and she planned to minimise those. These are outlined in Table 4.1 below.

Table 4.1. Potential difficulties for the children

Potential difficulty	Possible way(s) to prevent, overcome or address the difficulty
Level of computational skill required too high for some pupils.	Allow self-selecting groups (which has usually produced mixed attainment groups). Use of TA and teacher to support pupils as necessary.
Large amount of data that needs to be researched, recorded and used.	Provide some groups with a suggested template.
Time required to undertake the research.	At the beginning of the unit, discuss together the timescales involved. Explain what will happen when certain stages are not completed by the deadline.
Lack of interest in the task.	Enable pupils to decide on the product and the source (therefore giving autonomy to the decision-making).
Process is more important than product, in that there is no 'right answer'.	Explain at the outset that there is an acknowledgement that all solutions will be different. Costings will be dependent on quality, source, size, type, etc. It is important that all pupils are able to justify their decisions. Produce a prompt sheet for the Using and Applying Number skills for pupils to evaluate their process.

Toni's confidence in her pedagogical subject knowledge is evident in this case study as she competently allows self-selected groups of children to solve the problem she has set them. This involves a high level of classroom management (particularly use of resources by the children) but by doing so she is providing the children with a rich learning environment.

Toni's confidence in her mathematical subject knowledge is also evident. She is able to:

- understand groups' methods of recording, and suggest ways for them to refine their recording where necessary;
- clearly explain, using symbols, demonstration and children's use, how to use functions on the calculator that are new to them;
- recap on past learning and use this new situation to check children's understanding of other mathematical ideas (i.e. BODMAS);

- ask questions to elicit children's understanding of the problem-solving process, encouraging them to explain why they made some of the decisions they made;
- integrate using and applying number (Ma1) with Number (Ma2).

FURTHER READING
Clare Green has produced an interesting article about the use of calculators in schools on the NRich website at: http://nrich.maths.org/public/viewer.php?obj_id =2553

Different types of calculators are discussed in Chapter 1.

Using the calculator to assist children with solving problems

The positive features of calculator use listed at the beginning of this section can all be seen to some extent in this case study. Toni acknowledges that the pupils will be using mental calculation strategies at times alongside the use of the calculator. It is apparent that the children in this group have a positive attitude and high motivation towards mathematics. However, even with these children in this context, the calculator supports their problem-solving skills by enabling them to handle large volumes of data in a shorter period of time than if they had been required to use pencil and paper methods to calculate the solutions.

5
Understanding shape

Introduction

In order to understand shape, children need to be able to describe positioning and transformation of shapes, and recognise their properties to visualise and construct shapes appropriately. From the youngest age, shape has an intuitive appeal (French, 2004). Children develop ideas that can later lead to sophisticated geometrical understanding.

In this chapter we will look at five aspects of understanding shape:

1. *Position, direction and movement*. How do children make sense of their position in the world? How do everyday activities support mathematical development? This includes an Early Years Foundation Stage case study about a three-year old child who is talking about getting ready for school.

2. *2D and 3D shape*. How does the environment support children's understanding of the 3D and 2D world? How does manipulation of objects help children's geometrical understanding? This includes a Year 2 case study about children going on a shape hunt.

3. *Measuring a 'degree'*. Are there different ways of thinking about angles? How can children support each other in their learning? How can resources aid children to understand static and dynamic angles? This case study shows Year 4 children being introduced to acute, straight and obtuse angles.

4. *Transformational geometry*. What is rotation, reflection and translation? What is the difference between process and product? Why are both important? This includes a Year 5/6 case study about the class visiting a wallpaper manufacturer to develop their understanding of transformational geometry.

5. *Properties of triangles*. How can triangles be named and sorted? Why do children struggle to understand shape according to its properties? How can primary school children 'prove' their mathematical ideas? The case study in this section looks at Year 6/7 pupils sorting and classifying triangles according to some of their attributes.

1. Position, direction and movement

Propositional language is necessary for children to be able to position themselves, objects and shapes in our three-dimensional world (Greeno, 1980). Additionally, if children display a *lack* of propositional language, then it is likely that their visual learning can be constrained (Clements and Battista, 1992).

CASE STUDY: GETTING DOLLY READY FOR SCHOOL (EYFS)

Context

In this case study, Hayleigh is working with Sian who is three. Her sister has just started school and at nursery Sian is playing with a doll in the dolls' house getting it ready for school.

Curriculum Content

The Early Learning Goals

Problem Solving, Reasoning and Numeracy: Use language such as 'circle' or 'bigger' to describe the shape and size of solids and flat shapes.

Use everyday words to describe position.

Task

What is the value of modelling mathematical language to young children?

Hayleigh:	(*Observes Sian playing with the doll.*)
Sian:	Come on, school today. It's Monday so you go to school. Good girl. Wakey wakey, rise and shine. Breakfast time. (*Sian takes doll downstairs to the kitchen.*) Sit there. Good girl. You will have toast today. Do you want honey or jam, Olivia? I will make you some honey toast.
Hayleigh:	Are you making Olivia some toast?
Sian:	Yes.
Hayleigh:	What spread is she having on top of it?
Sian:	Honey toast.
Hayleigh:	Can I help you?
Sian:	No. I do it.
Hayleigh:	OK. How are you making the toast?
Sian:	The bread goes (*she curls herself up in to a ball*) and pop (*she jumps up and yells 'pop'*) and then me butter and put jam.
Hayleigh:	Where do you get the butter and jam from?
Sian:	Fridge.
Hayleigh:	The butter and the jam are both in the fridge?
Sian:	Yes.
Hayleigh:	And are you spreading the jam and the butter on the top of the toast?
Sian:	No. Me put the butter on first. (*Spreads the play bread with pretend butter and then jam using a play knife.*)
Hayleigh:	Oh, of course you do! Silly me.
Sian:	Here you are Olivia. This is your plate. (*Feeds doll the toast.*) Yum yum. Good girl, Olivia.
Hayleigh:	Can I have some toast with Olivia, please?
Sian:	Me make you some.
Hayleigh:	Thank you. Can I have jam, please? What sort of jam do you have in your fridge?
Sian:	Pink.
Hayleigh:	Pink jam? I like that. Can I have a plate for my toast too?
Sian:	Here your plate. Your plate grown-up plate and Olivia's a baby plate.

Hayleigh:	I see. So is my plate bigger or smaller than Olivia's?
Sian:	It's a big, big plate. 'Cos Olivia is a baby. She has a little, little plate. When I grow up, up, up to the ceiling I'm going to have a big, big, big, big, big, big plate, just like you. You ate up your breakfast. You can go to school now.
Hayleigh:	How can we get to school?
Sian:	The bus!
Hayleigh:	Olivia goes to school on the bus?
Sian:	Double decker bus.
Hayleigh:	I see. Does she sit at the top of the bus or at the bottom of the bus?
Sian:	She goes on the top at the front.
Hayleigh:	I like sitting on the top at the front. You can see everything around you.
Sian:	Me too. (*Takes Olivia and sings 'The Wheels on the Bus' followed by 'Today is Monday and we're going to school'.*)

Extending subject knowledge

Using propositional language to describe everyday activities

Sian, who is three, is currently very interested in school because of her sister's recent move to junior school and her knowledge that she will go to school when she is four. When Hayleigh began to observe Sian, she listened carefully to the language she was using. Hayleigh noticed that while she was making references to the time of day ('wakey wakey', 'breakfast time') and the day of the week ('It's Monday so you go to school'), Sian had not used any propositional language (e.g. get *out* of bed, put honey *on* the toast, go *down* the stairs, etc.). At this point, Hayleigh began to use propositional language herself ('what spread is she having *on* it?', '*in* the fridge') in order to assess Sian's use and understanding of such terminology.

Read more about observation in Chapter 3.

Early in the conversation, Sian used few propositions. She stated that she would 'put the butter on first', but then the focus changes to the size of the plates. Later, however, Sian articulately explains the position of her doll on the double decker bus: 'She goes on the top at the front'.

2. 2D and 3D shape

The environment is the obvious starting point for supporting children's understanding of 3D and 2D shape and space. After all, the names of two-dimensional shapes were created to help explain and describe the three-dimensional world in which we live. Much research demonstrates that the best way for young children to learn about shape is in a hands-on environment (Reys et al., 2006). Yet to focus only on the shapes we find in our environment can be misleading to children. For example, when a 'kite' is mentioned to children, they immediately visualise the prototypical shape of the toy that can be found flying in the sky. Having only these representations of shapes means

that children develop very limited understanding of shape (Hershkowitz, 1990). And these strong mental images often remain (Hershkowitz et al., 1990).

Children often have difficulty moving to 2-D representations from a 3-D environment. Many suggest the use of dynamic geometry software as an effective way for older primary school children to develop their understanding of the properties of shapes. Furner and Marinas (2007) used one version of this software (*Geometer's Sketchpad*) in a number of contexts with Kindergarten to Grade 4 children and reported that the Grade 2 children were able to use the software with ease.

CASE STUDY: SHAPE HUNT (YEAR 2)

Context
In this case study, Leah, the class teacher, is explaining the value of the photographs her pupils took as they went on a shape hunt around the school.

Curriculum Content
National Curriculum Key Stage 1
Pupils should be taught to:

Ma3.2a: describe properties of shapes that they can see or visualise using the related vocabulary.

Ma3.2b: observe, handle and describe common 2D and 3D shapes; name and describe the mathematical features of common 2D and 3D shapes...

Primary Framework Year 2
Visualise common 2D shapes and 3D solids; identify shapes from pictures of them in different positions and orientations; sort, make and describe shapes, referring to their properties.

Task
How does technology used in this way support the children's understanding of shape?

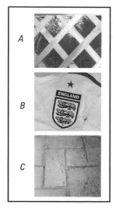
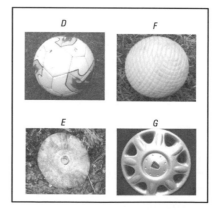

I have a number of children in my class with a variety of special educational needs and there is also a wide spread of attainment within the class. Part of my reason for going out on the shape hunt yesterday was to encourage the children to talk to each other and their accompanying adult about the shapes

they could see around the school. The children participated as I'd expected them to. They were interested in their surroundings and they got really excited when they were the first to find a new shape or a 3D solid, and they were really interested in all the names.

We took hundreds of photos! I spent most of last night editing them – they're not the best photographers, my lot! *(Laughs.)* But it was worth it. This morning they looked at their photos and I asked them to group them, firstly according to their own criteria and then, later, to some mathematical criteria. I'd put some ideas up on the board for them as prompts.

I wanted to show you this grouping that some of my lower attainment children have done. They grouped them, as I'm sure you can tell, into shapes that roll, and shapes that don't roll. On the face of it I thought, 'Well, that is pretty much what I expected. You have been able to identify the curved faces as those are the ones that roll'. But, when I spoke to Margaret, our teaching assistant, about their discussion, I was blown away!

For a start, they discussed what they meant by rolling. The logo on this t-shirt here (Picture B) produced some discussion about the shapes – a star, a rectangle, a shield – but the most interesting part was about what it meant to roll. One of the children suggested that it could roll, because the child wearing it could roll around on the floor! So Margaret talked to them about the curved faces.

Their attention was then drawn to the football (Picture D). Some of them thought that it was called a sphere, although some of them called it a Sophia! Margaret pointed out the hexagons and pentagons. Some of them had heard those names before. They identified which were pentagons and which were hexagons. They counted the number of sides. Margaret explained to them that a sphere can't have any faces on it like this football does and that this wasn't actually a sphere. She showed them another example of a smooth plastic ball in the class that was, so they could compare them. When one of them asked what it was called, she told them: an icosadodecahedron. They loved that! They're into names of dinosaurs and all sorts of thing at that age, aren't they, and these were no different!

And there were loads of other words describing polygons and polyhedra being used. They talked about the concentric circles in the tree log (Picture E) and how to tell the age of a tree by doing that. They also looked at the circles etched around that blue ball (Picture F). When Margaret told me about that, I thought I'd try to get some sliceforms to show them. That reminded me of those.

Transcript from discussion with Leah, Year 2 class teacher.

REMINDER
An icosadodecahedron, or (20,12)-hedron, is so called because it has 20 faces of one type and 12 of another. The football has 20 hexagons and 12 pentagons.

RELATED VIEWING
It is possible to watch the interview of John Sharp, the author of many books about sliceforms, at www.lkl.ac.uk/video/sharp0306interview.html

Using Venn diagrams is a way to sort data. To read more about handling data read Chapter 7.

Extending subject knowledge

Using manipulation and sorting to support geometrical development

The teaching assistant in this case study was very enthusiastic about using the environment to teach mathematical ideas. Additionally, she was adamant that the children she worked with, regardless of their attainment level, should participate in lessons appropriately, by listening and having the opportunity to use a range of mathematical vocabulary that stimulates and challenges their interest in mathematics. The importance of children using correct geometrical language has been well-documented (Anghilieri and Baron, 1999; Garrick, 2002; Hasegawa, 1997; Saads and Davis, 1997). Saads and Davis (1997, p17) explain that *discussion involving the names and characteristics of the 3-D shapes is necessary for children to clarify mathematical understanding, for example in the relationships between cubes and squares* ...

The class teacher was also an enthusiastic teacher of mathematics. She had discussed with her teaching assistant what the children had learnt in that lesson with the intention of building on it in further tasks and activities. By thinking about the resources that she could use to stimulate their thought – such as using slice-forms – she was explicitly creating situations where the children could manipulate shapes that were different from the prototypical shapes they were accustomed to in their environment (Hershkowitz, 1990). She was also exploring the creative nature of mathematics.

3. Measuring a 'degree'

Lehrer et al. (1998) outline three ways an angle can be perceived. The first is by *movement*, for example a rotation. The second is *in a geometric shape* created by two intersecting lines. The final is a bringing together these first two. It is a *measure*.

In their study, Lehrer et al. (1998, p164) found that children did not tend to see angles as a movement (a turn or sweep). However, they did find that from a young age children were able to separate angles from a figure. This capacity suggests that many young children are doing more than simply noting that figures 'have corners'. Instead, they appear to reliably distinguish among (at least some) angles of measure, and they can mentally decompose a two-dimensional figure into separate attributes of length and angle.

CASE STUDY: 'THAT'S A CUTE ANGLE!' (YEAR 4)
Context
In this case study, Rosemary is exploring different sized angles with her pupils. During the introduction to the lesson she reviewed 'right' and 'straight' angles with them, and introduced the terms 'acute' and 'obtuse' angles. In the main part of the lesson, the pupils are asked, in small groups, to circle, using particular colours, the acute, right and obtuse angles on the angles identification sheet (see Figure 5.1). The transcript below is from a discussion between two pupils.

Curriculum Content
National Curriculum Key Stage 2
Pupils should be taught to:

Ma3.4c: recognise angles as greater or less than a right angle or half-turn, estimate their size and order them ...

Primary Framework Year 4
Know that angles are measured in degrees and that one whole turn is 360°;
compare and order angles less than 180°.

Task
The angles are displayed on the sheet in a range of orientations. Why do you
think that this is necessary?

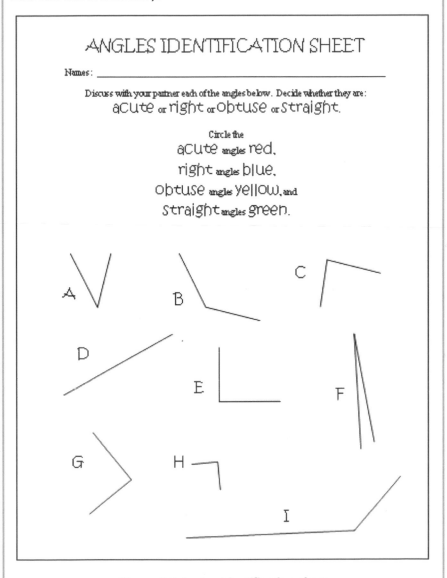

Figure 5.1 Angles identification sheet

Tessa:	The first one is acute. That's easy
Georgina:	How did you know that?
Tessa:	'Cos it is smaller than a right angle. I'll circle it red.
Georgina:	F is a cute angle too.
Tessa:	(*Laughs.*) Not a 'cute' angle, silly! Acute.
Georgina:	That's what I said!

Tessa:	No, you said it was a 'cute' angle! It is *an acute angle*, not a (*pause*) 'cute' angle
Georgina:	Oh.
Tessa:	What about B?
Georgina:	That's the big one. What's it called?
Tessa:	Let me check. (*Looks at sheet.*) Oh, it is obtuse.
Georgina:	Obtuse?
Tessa:	Obtuse … that's yellow.
Georgina:	I'll do it.
Tessa:	OK.
Georgina:	(*Circles the angle.*) I'll never learn these names.
Tessa:	It is easy.
Georgina:	For you maybe.
Tessa:	You know right angle.
Georgina:	Yeah.
Tessa:	And straight is easy like Miss said, 'cos it is just a straight line.
Georgina:	Yeah, but the other acute and ob-, ob-, ob- thingee is hard and I get them mixed up.
Tessa:	Well, what's that one? (*Points to angle F.*)
Georgina:	It is the little one.
Tessa:	Acute one.
Georgina:	If you think so.
Tessa:	Huh?
Georgina:	Well, if you think it's cute!
Tessa:	No! It is an acute angle. But it is cute too, 'cos it's small.
Georgina:	That's it! I can remember it like that. A cute angle is small so it is acute! Haha.
Tessa:	What about obtuse.
Georgina:	That one. (*Points to angle B.*)
Tessa:	Yeah, but how will you remember that? Obtuse?
Georgina:	Maybe because it is big it is obvious so that is obtuse.
Tessa:	Obvious?
Georgina:	Obtuse and obvious. They both start with ob.
Tessa:	Oh yeah, good one. Shall we tell Miss?
Georgina:	Yeah!

Extending subject knowledge

Using children to support others' learning

The girls' teacher designed the sheet to stimulate discussion. Her main aim, as it happens, was to encourage discussion about right angles and near right angles, with decisions being made on whether particular angles were acute, right or obtuse. She wanted to encourage the children to use various strategies to work out the names of the angles. Thus her design of the worksheet included several angles that were close to 90°.

However, these two children first spent time solving their own problem. Georgina was concerned that she was unable to remember the names of the different types of angles, and Tessa set about to help her remember them. On informing their teacher of their tip, the lesson was interrupted for the girls to share their idea. This was taken up by some of the children.

Their teacher developed this idea with a group of higher attainment children later when they were introduced to the reflex angle. They used the word r*eflex* to think about *flex*ible people who can bend themselves in unusual ways and that this angle was *flex*ible because it could move further than 180°.

Using resources to develop children's understanding of static and dynamic angles

In addition to using the children's ideas for remembering the angle labels, the teacher used a dynamic model to show the children the angles. It was simply constructed out of two strips of card ajoined by a split pin. This enabled the pupils to see one way that an angle might be produced and it helped them to see that degrees were used to measure the angle (Lehrer et al., 1998). A great deal of evidence has shown that part of children's difficulty with understanding angle is their inability to view angles as dynamic (Noss, 1987). Indeed, most work undertaken in school is paper-based and reinforces angles as static. The teacher was aware that the sheet provided as a discussion point for the pupils in the case study presented the children with static angle images, albeit that they were presented in various rotations. Using the home-made resource to broaden the models used with (and images formed by) the children was intentional.

4. Transformational geometry

Rotation, reflection and translation are all types of transformations that describe movement. They can be broadly grouped with enlargement under the heading of transformational geometry.

CASE STUDY: A VISIT TO THE WALLPAPER MANUFACTURER (YEAR 5/6)

Context

In this case study, Pete has already taken his class to the wallpaper manufacturer as an introduction to the next unit which includes looking at patterns with rotational and reflective symmetry in them. Below are three samples of children's work that were completed on a simple computer drawing program ('Paint') after their visit to the factory. They were able to develop their ICT skills as well as discuss the transformational geometry techniques they were utilising to create their own wallpaper for their room. They were required to write a commentary about their work in a word processing package for a display of their work on the wall and also to send it to the tour guide at the wallpaper manufacturing company. The teacher's assessment notes and evaluation of the lesson follow the samples.

FURTHER READING
You can read about rotation, reflection and translation in Chapter 5 of Mooney et al. (2007) *Primary mathematics: knowledge and understanding*. Exeter: Learning Matters.

Curriculum Content
National Curriculum Key Stage 2
Pupils should be taught to:

Ma3.1e: recognise simple spatial patterns and relationships and make predictions about them.

Ma3.3b: transform objects in practical situations; transform images using ICT; visualise and predict the position of a shape following a rotation, reflection or translation.

<u>*Primary Framework Year 5*</u>

Complete patterns with up to two lines of symmetry; draw the position of a shape after a reflection or translation.

<u>*Primary Framework Year 6*</u>

Visualise and draw on grids of different types where a shape will be after reflection, after translation, or after rotation through 90° or 180° about its centre or one of its vertices.

Task

What other contexts could you use to develop children's appreciation of transformational geometry in life?

I made my initial pattern and then rotated it 180° around point A.
Then I translated it all over the page.

Mark

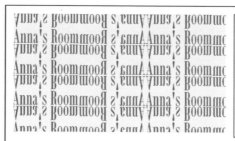

Anna's Room

I made my template and then I reflected it in a mirror line under my name. Then I translated it. I put the lemon background on after and it was hard colouring in all the spaces in the letters. Now I have evaluated my work I would like to keep reflecting it to see what happens.

Anna Robinson

This was my first tree. Then I made a whole forest of trees by copying and pasting and making them bigger or smaller.

Then I copied and pasted the forest all over.

Terence

Assessment notes		
Name	**Comment**	**Points for development**
Anna	Uses some terminology effectively: reflected, mirrorline, translated. Thoughtful evaluation discussed with me, but she did not write it all down.	Encourage Anna to use 'line of reflection' now. Give her the opportunity to try out her idea for a different design.
Mark	Mark identified the point around which his pattern was rotated. Got particularly excited by the fact that there are only 17 mathematically different wallpaper designs.	Encourage him to think about other transformations that could have been used to produce the same product (e.g. more rotation around other points). Research with Mark some websites that explain the 17 different designs of wallpapers – see how far he gets!
Terence	Terry is confident with the notion of enlargement and reduction, although he is still referring to it as making it 'bigger' and 'smaller'.	Talk to Terry about the difference between a picture and a pattern. Reinforce mathematical terminology of enlargement and reduction and encourage him to use those terms.
Lesson evaluation		

5 & 6 June

The majority of the children were able to use 'Paint' to create and design their wallpaper.

It was helpful to tell them the day before what we were going to do so they came with some ideas.

Timing the lesson so that the children had to work with what they had created by the end of the first lesson was helpful because it focused them.

The TA was very helpful reinforcing language to all the pupils as needed and also supporting them with the technology when needed.

It was very useful visiting the factory prior to starting their work and also having Mike ask them to send him their designs. This made the children far more interested and focused them more than last year's class who didn't see the point as much.

This year they tended to stick with the first idea that came into their head or that they did on the computer. Next time, spend three days (not two) on this and have the middle day away from the computers where they use their template to draft a number of possible wallpaper designs on paper. This will help reinforce reflection, rotation, translation further.

Explore links with DT as well as ICT and art.

Extending subject knowledge

Asking children to share their process and product with others

In my experience, when children have an *audience* for carrying out their maths work (such as sending their findings to the wallpaper company, or the local police officer – see Chapter 1), the quality of their work (both their mathematical thinking through the process and their product) improves. Too often mathematics is carried out in a secret world: a book task is completed for the teacher to mark and then it is returned to a tray. If the only audience is the teacher and the pupil, then this constrains the reasons why the pupil may carry out the work and, in longer

You can read more about having a sense of audience in Chapter 7.

term, I suggest this could have a negative effect on their interest and motivation in mathematics.

In this case study, Pete has a similar view on the value that he places on his pupils' work. He generally encourages them to produce their best work by displaying every pupil's work whenever it is possiblee. However, his reasons for doing this are more than to encourage children to finish their work, make it neat and create an attractive classroom. His focus remains fully on the mathematics that the children are using as part of their work. He does this in several ways.

- He had spoken with the tour guide and his TA prior to the unit of work, explaining the expectations he had for the children and the language he was introducing to them and expecting them to use. He also gave them both an overview of the unit so that everyone knew what the purpose of the unit (and the visit in particular) was.
- The work that the children displayed required them to explain the processes they carried out (they were encouraged to use correct mathematical terminology in this).
- By displaying the pupils' products, terminology is reinforced every time the children read each other's work.
- He introduced the unit of work to the children, outlining the content and the objectives. He encouraged the children to bring in examples of patterns from other contexts. The children responded with a range of artefacts such as fabrics, wrapping paper, tiles, plastic cup motifs, hand-made quilts, etc.
- His assessments of the children's work (during the process and the product) were insightful and remained focused on the mathematical elements (he completed a separate assessment for ICT). Additionally, he had thought about each pupil's areas of development and jotted these down.
- Pete's evaluation of the two days in the computer suite helped him to think about how his planning supported the children's mathematical development and also how he would amend it if he repeated it with another group of children.

5. Properties of triangles

One way to define a triangle is as a polygon with three vertices (thus the name: *tri*-angle). It is also possible to name triangles according to the length of their sides (equilateral, isosceles or scalene), or their internal angles (acute, right-angled or obtuse). Polygons can be also defined by other attributes, such as their lines of reflection, order of rotation, number of pairs of equal and opposite angles or number of parallel sides.

Fischbein (1993, 1994) reminds us how complex geometry is. He explains that geometry is different from other mathematical concepts because when a person has an understanding of a particular shape it involves a personal mental image sitting alongside the person's known properties of that shape. For example, if someone mentions a 'square' to you, you will immediately picture a square in your mind (probably a prototypical one, with a horizontal base). But alongside that, you may also know that it is a regular quadrilateral, it has an order of rotation of four, it has four lines of symmetry, it has two pairs of parallel sides, it has perpendicular diagonals (which bisect) and it has two sets of equal and opposite angles (which all happen to be right angles). Because the *figure* interacts with the *conceptual* aspects, Fischbein (1994) refers to this as a *figural concept*. He believes that a child develops their insight into figural concepts of shapes as they get older and as they participate in effective learning situations.

CASE STUDY: CAN YOU DRAW A RIGHT-ANGLED, EQUILATERAL TRIANGLE? (YEARS 6/7)

Context
In this case study, Lisa's class are at the end of their unit of work which has involved a lot of discussion about the types of triangles: acute, right, obtuse, equilateral, isosceles and scalene. She has given them a choice of final problems. One of them is below. It is being worked through by one mixed-attainment group of boys.

Curriculum Content
National Curriculum Key Stage 2
Pupils should be taught to:

Ma3.1d: use checking procedures to confirm that their results of geometrical problems are reasonable.

Ma3.2b: visualise and describe 2D and 3D shapes and the way they behave, making more precise use of geometrical language, especially that of triangles.

Primary Framework Year 6/7
Extend knowledge of properties of triangles and quadrilaterals and use these to visualise and solve problems, explaining reasoning with diagrams.

Task
How does focusing on a small number of attributes help support children to develop their definitions of shapes?

DRAWING TRIANGLES

It is possible to draw triangles according to the SIZE of their ANGLES: acute, right-angled and obtuse.

It is also possible to draw triangles according to the LENGTH of their SIDES: equilateral, isosceles and scalene.

BUT ...

Is it possible to draw triangles so that they are named according to BOTH? (For example, can you draw an acute isosceles triangle? Or a right-angled scalene triangle?)

Are there any triangles that are impossible? If so, WHY?

Make sure you record your thinking effectively!

Leigh:	I can imagine a few. Like an acute isosceles triangle. That's easy – it is like that. (*Draws an acute isosceles triangle.*)
Sinead:	Yeah. And you can do a right-angled scalene triangle because you just have to make all the sides different lengths and include one right angle only.
Leigh:	Yeah. But are there any impossible ones? What about, um, I can't do a right-angled isosceles triangle.
Sinead:	Can't you?
Leigh:	No.
Sinead:	Why not?
Leigh:	Because it is impossible.
Sinead:	Why?
Leigh:	You can't draw the sides long enough if you make one angle a right angle.
Sinead:	Yes you can. And the sides that come out from the right angle are the two that are the same length. (*Draws a right-angled isosceles triangle.*)
Leigh:	Ahhhh! Oh yeah. OK, so which one is impossible?
Sinead:	I don't know. I think you can do all of them.
Leigh:	So why does it say to say why it is impossible? It wouldn't ask that if there wasn't any that you couldn't do.
Sinead:	Well then, do a chart and let's see.
Leigh:	What?
Sinead:	Do it this way. (*Draws the following chart and together they fill it in.*)

	Equilateral	Isosceles	Scalene
Acute			
Right-angled	✖		
Obtuse	✖		

Sinead:	There we go, then. You really can't do a right-angled equilateral triangle or an obtuse equilateral triangle.
Lisa:	(*Arrives.*) What have you two been finding out, then?
Sinead:	We have been looking at all the triangles to see which ones we can and can't make.
Lisa:	And what have you found out?
Sinead:	You can't make a right-angled equilateral triangle or an obtuse right-angled triangle.
Lisa:	So why not, then?
Sinead:	Well an equilateral triangle has all the same length sides and we couldn't draw any that had the same length sides.

Lisa:	OK. But how do you know that you just haven't yet thought of one, and that really there are such things as those types of equilateral triangles?
Leigh:	Yeah! That's what I said.
Lisa:	Well, do you think you know why, Leigh?
Leigh:	Well, we did it in a table to help us.
Lisa:	Why did you decide to use a Carroll diagram, like this?
Sinead:	Because then you can see easily the two types you are trying to make. See, this first one is equilateral because all the sides are the same length, and it is also acute because all of the angles are less than 90°.
Lisa:	Good, so you have found examples that satisfy each of those, but not the two that are left. Can you think of any other logical reasons why you would not be able to construct them? You have been talking about the length of the sides in equilateral triangles, but there is another property that sets them aside from the rest.
Leigh:	Oooh, I know. The angles. They have the same angles.
Lisa:	And how many degrees are there in each angle?
Sinead:	They are 60°. All of them. They all add up to 180° and they are all equal and 180° divided by three gives 60°.
Lisa:	And so how might that knowledge help us to answer why we can't make these two types of triangles?
Sinead:	Oh, because a right-angled triangle has to have a right angle and an equilateral triangle can't. And that's the same for an obtuse. It can't have any obtuse angles 'cos they're all 60.
Lisa:	Well done! Now I see that you have drawn all the possible triangles. Most of them have something in common. What is it?
Leigh:	They all have a flat bottom.
Lisa:	Yes, they have a horizontal base. Could I challenge you to draw some more, this time on the computer, that don't have a horizontal base? You could use the rotate function on the shapes to help you with that. See if you can make one more of each type to start with, but then see how many you can make of each one in the time we have left this morning. We'll show your work on the interactive white board at ten minutes to twelve, so please have it ready by then.
Girls:	OK! Thank you!

Extending subject knowledge

Challenging the impossible: beginning to think about proof

The girls were confident in their understanding of what the different triangles (acute, right-angled, obtuse, or equilateral, isosceles, scalene) looked like and how they were defined, either by their angles or sides. Lisa brought their knowledge of the properties of the two types of shapes together in this task, which enabled them to begin to see certain relationships between the angles and side lengths. Geometry helps us to develop the skills of reasoning (French, 2004) and the girls used logic and reasoning to explain their proof.

FURTHER READING
You can read more about language, reasoning and proof in Chapter 7 of Mooney et al. (2007) *Primary mathematics: knowledge and understanding.* Exeter: Learning Matters.

Going beyond current understanding

Lisa was impressed by the two girls' use of the definitions of the six different types of triangles. They were able to discuss the properties of the triangles succinctly and efficiently: two aspects essential to defining shapes. However, Lisa noticed that the girls were constructing mainly prototypical figures: the vast majority of the figures they drew developed from a horizontal baseline. Lisa had undertaken this task herself during her teacher training course, and she understood how surprisingly difficult it is to produce examples of each of the triangles in the Carroll diagram. By challenging the children to create more examples, she was demanding something of them that she felt was particularly challenging. However, by using technology, this was going to be far simpler. She knew that once the girls had produced one example, they would be able to clone it and simply change the size, rotate or skew it etc. to produce many different examples of the same type of triangle. Lisa knew that the girls discussing their successful (and unsuccessful) figures through this process would continue to develop their understanding of the classification of triangles.

6
Measuring

Introduction

Measurement was developed by humans through the necessity during activities such as trading and bartering for essential materials and goods. The ancient civilisations of the third and fourth centuries BC (for example, the Egyptians and the Babylonians), were the first to base their measurement systems on weights and measures. Weights were measured using seeds. The *carat*, used for weighing diamonds, measuring gold, etc. (equivalent to 200 grams) is derived from the ancient use of carob seeds. They used parts of their bodies and items from their environment to measure length. For example, the *cubit* was the length from the elbow to the tip of the index finger. Although it was not a standard length (everyone's arms vary in length!), it was a convenient tool to use and it is thought that the inch, foot and yard evolved from the cubit.

The first known civilisation to use a standard length measure was the Harappan Civilisation (2600–1900 BC), who lived in the Indus and Ghaggar-Hakra river valleys, in a region now including Pakistan, western India and east Balochistan. Archaeologists have found measures for length that are very small and precise, approximately 1.704mm, and weights of a unit approximately 28 grams. This made their measurement system very precise (Chakrabarti, 2004).

FURTHER READING
To read how the history of measurement is reflected in pupils' mathematical progression, read pages 145–9 of Mooney et al. (2007) *Primary mathematics: teaching theory and practice*. Exeter: Learning Matters.

In the modern world, measurement is used constantly within everything that we do. However, Nickson (2004, p35) warns us that, although measurement may be more accessible for children than many other aspects of mathematics, it is *an exceedingly complicated concept*.

Robinson's (2007) fascinating and beautifully presented book outlines the history, mathematics and tools of measurement and also considers how nature and man are measured. Some measurements in nature are very small (quantum theory) and others are very large (the heliocentric universe). Measures of man include the mind (e.g. library classification and IQ), the body (e.g. sun protection factors and medical prescriptions) and society (e.g. calendars, postal codes).

In this chapter we will look at five aspects of measurement.

1. *Progression in measurement.* What stages do children progress through in their understanding of all types of measurement? How can task design support children's progression in measurement? This section includes a case study about a Year 1 class beginning to use non-standard measures to compare objects.

2. *Reading scales.* Why is measurement only an approximation? How can careful resource selection support children learning to read scales? What is the difference between mass and weight? The case study involves two starters using the same resource, an Interactive Teaching Programme. One is with a Year 2 class and the other is with a Year 5 class.

3. *Relationships between km, m, cm; kg, g; l, ml.* What is the relationship between measures of the same attribute? How can practical activities support children in learning the relationship between measures? As well as converting, how can I support children in understanding measures as a concept? This section includes a Year 4 case study about a class demonstrating how many millilitres are in a litre.

4. *Estimating length.* Why are estimation skills important? Why should we plan some of our mathematics lessons to run outside the classroom? What is an estimation? How can I support children in developing their estimation skills? This section includes a Year 4 case study about a group estimating the length of dinosaurs.

5. *Perimeter and area.* How can children explore the relation between perimeter and area? What methods can be used to calculate the area of rectilinear and irregular shapes? How can the area of a circle be calculated when I know only the circumference? This section includes a Year 6 investigation of shapes with a constant perimeter.

1. Progression in measurement

There is a clear progression that children take in measurement, regardless of the attribute that is involved. This progression mirrors the evolution of measurement through the history of humankind.

Progression in measurement
1. There is a need to understand the *attribute* that is being measured: length, mass, capacity, perimeter, area, angle, time.
2. Direct comparison:
   (a) of two objects;
   (b) of three objects;
   (c) ordering a set of objects.
3. Comparison using units:
   (a) arbitrary units (of arbitrary size, e.g. buttons, leaves);
   (b) non-standard units (of uniform size, e.g. multi-link cubes, an individual's hand span).
4. Use of standards units.
5. Conversions of standard units:
   (a) metric → metric;
   (b) imperial ←→ metric.

Throughout this progression it is necessary for children to continuously estimate and discuss their estimations.

CASE STUDY: THE THREE BEARS (YEAR 1)

Context

In this case study, the termly topic in the Year 1 class is bears. The teacher, Kirsty, has spread some items belonging to the bears around the classroom. She is going to task the children with finding out which item belongs to each bear (Daddy Bear, Mummy Bear and Baby Bear) but because they are so spread apart the children are unable to undertake a direct comparison of the objects.

Curriculum Content

Ma3.4a: estimate the size of objects compare and measure objects using

<u>National Curriculum Key Stage 1</u>
Pupils should be taught to:

Ma3.4a: estimate the size of objects compare and measure objects using uniform non-standard units...

<u>Primary Framework Year 1</u>
Estimate, measure, weigh and compare objects, choosing and using suitable uniform non-standard or standard units and measuring instruments.

Task

How does task design impact on children meeting the learning outcomes of your lessons?

Kirsty:	So what item would you like to find for Daddy Bear first?
Jeremy:	The bowl!
Kirsty:	OK, can you all see the three bowls that Goldilocks has hidden around the classroom?
All:	(*The children point to the three bowls, which are clearly visible, but in different locations around the classroom.*)
Kirsty:	Good. Which one do you think belongs to Daddy Bear?
All:	(*There is a disagreement between two of the bowls belonging to Daddy Bear.*)
Kirsty:	How might we decide which one is Daddy Bear's, and which one belongs to Mummy Bear?
Ian:	Put them next to each other and see.
Kirsty:	We could, Ian, but remember Goldilocks told us in her note that we were not allowed to do that!
Rory:	We could put some porridge in both and see which had more in it.
Kirsty:	That's a great idea, Rory! Oh! But I haven't brought any porridge to school. What do you think we could use instead?
Rory:	Marbles.
Kirsty:	OK, shall we use marbles to see which bowl is the biggest?
All:	Yes.
Kirsty:	The bowl that is the biggest will hold the most marbles. Rory, could you go over by that bowl there with Miss Hewson and fill the bowl with the marbles?
Rory:	Yes. (*Rory follows Kirsty's instructions and with the teaching assistant's help, fills the bowl.*)

Kirsty:	Well done. Can I have another person to fill the second bowl with marbles? Thank you Laura.
Laura:	(*Completes the task with the teaching assistant.*)
Kirsty:	We have filled the two bowls with marbles. What do we have to now?
Wendy:	We have to count the marbles and see which one has more.
Kirsty:	Well done, Wendy. Before we do that, who thinks Rory's bowl is the biggest? (*A show of hands go up.*) And Laura's? (*Another show of hands.*) OK! Let's see which bowl holds the most marbles. Rory, would you like to count your marbles?
Rory:	(*With help from the teaching assistant.*) 1, 2, 3, 4, 5, ... 27, 28.
Kirsty:	Twenty-eight! Thank you Rory. (*Writes '28' on the board.*) Your turn, Laura.
Laura:	(*Independently.*) 1, 2, 3, 4, 5, ... 21, 22.
Kirsty:	So you have 22 marbles in your bowl, Laura. Thank you. (*Writes '22' on the board. Several hands have already gone up.*) Who thinks they can tell us which bowl is Daddy Bear's bowl? Jamie?
Jamie:	That one (*Points to the bowl by Rory.*)
Kirsty:	And why is that, Jamie?
Jamie:	Because it had more marbles in it so it is the biggest one.

Extending subject knowledge

Using non-standard measures to compare two objects

Kirsty was aware that many of the children in her class were competent at directly comparing two objects. She constructed the task in this lesson so that the children had to think about how they could undertake a comparison in a different way. She thought that this would help them to begin to make comparisons using units and this worked effectively.

Kirsty had cleverly constructed a story so that the children were unable to directly compare the objects: the letter from Goldilocks (which had been found by the teaching assistant and read to the class). The idea of using an independent item to compare the two bowls came from the children through her questioning. The children chose marbles to compare the capacity of the two bowls they were unsure about (it was obvious to the children that the third was a lot smaller). To develop the children's understanding of what capacity is measuring further, Kirsty could have encouraged the children to estimate how many marbles they thought each bowl could hold prior to this being carried out.

The task continued with the children using other non-standard items to compare the height of the chairs (felt tips) and the area of the duvet covers from the beds (A4 paper). Once decisions had been made about which items belonged to each bear, they were brought together for the children to have the opportunity to order them using direct comparison. This confirmed their findings and helped the children to reflect on the method of comparison they had been introduced to.

2. Reading scales

When we measure something, the number we assign it (e.g. 46 seconds, 3.99 metres, 3,021 grams) is only an approximation to the actual measurement. The context in which we work has a bearing on how specific we are required to be when we read the scales of the measurements we take. For example, I am content knowing that I have run a 10km fun run in under one and a quarter hours, but 10,000m athletes such as Paula Radcliffe constantly strive to improve their personal best (which at the time of writing was 30:01.09 and the European Record).

Even when we measure something as accurately as this, in hundredths of a second, this is still only an approximation to the *actual* time that Paula crossed that line. It is something that can never be measured accurately because it we do not have the technology to do so. Indeed, no measurements can be recorded exactly. Regardless of the unit we are measuring in, only an approximation of the measurement is being undertaken.

> REMINDER
> Time uses a number of bases. There are 24 hours in a day, 60 minutes in an hour, 60 seconds in a minute, then tenths and hundredths of seconds! Fractions of time were decimalised as we developed the technology to measure them precisely.

CASE STUDY: READING SCALES (YEAR 2 AND YEAR 5)

Context
In these two case studies, the PPA teacher, Teresa, has been asked to teach mathematics lessons to the Year 2 class and the Year 5 class. Her starters for each of the lessons will use the same resource, an interactive teaching programme (ITP) using scales. She will vary the level of the work with the children by changing the numbers and the divisions on the scales.

Curriculum Content Year 2 Case Study
National Curriculum Key Stage 1
Pupils should be taught to:

Ma3.4c: estimate, measure and weigh objects; choose and use simple measuring instruments, reading and interpreting numbers, and scales to the nearest labelled division.

PNS Framework for mathematics
Year 2: Read the numbered divisions on a scale, and interpret the divisions between them.

Curriculum Content Year 5 Case Study
National Curriculum Key Stage 2
Pupils should be taught to:

Ma3.4b: Read scales with increasing accuracy; record measurement using decimal notation.

PNS Framework for mathematics
Year 5: Interpret a reading that lies between two unnumbered divisions on a scale.

Task
What are the advantages and disadvantages of using a resource like an ITP with the whole class?

Excerpt from Teresa's starter with the Year 2 class:

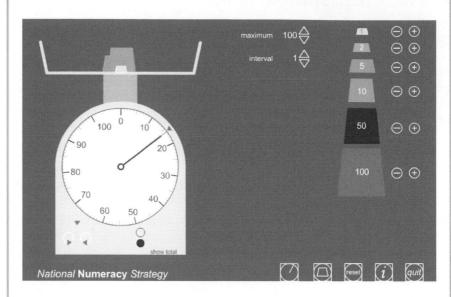

Teresa:	Well done, Stephanie. The scales are pointing to the 16. Sixteen kilograms. How did you know that?
Stephanie:	I could see that the line was one mark after the green one, which is fifteen.
Teresa:	And so you counted on one more kilogram?
Stephanie:	Yes.
Teresa:	Thank you. That is very good thinking, Stephanie. Who else knew that the scales were showing us 16 kilograms? (*Several hands go up.*)
Teresa:	Who used a different way to work out the answer? Antony?
Antony:	I counted back from 20.
Teresa:	Can you come up and show us all, please?
Antony:	(*Points to the 20, then along the divisions as he counts back in ones.*) 19, 18, 17, 16.
Teresa:	Who else did it that way? (*Some hands go up.*)
Teresa:	Do we have any other ways people worked out the reading? David?
David:	I counted from the ten up to sixteen.
Teresa:	I see. Thank you David. Did you *have* to count all the way up from ten, or was there another number that you could have counted up from that would make your working out faster and maybe more reliable?
David:	The five.
Teresa:	Yes, David, I see what you mean. But is it really a five?
David:	Oh, no, I mean fifteen.
Teresa:	Well done.

Excerpt from Teresa's starter with the Year 5 class:

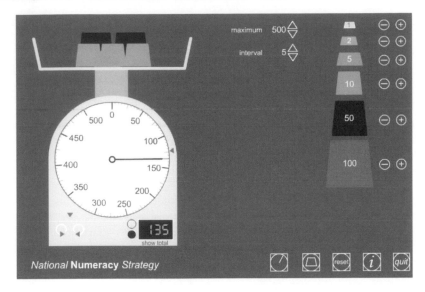

Teresa:	Let's try another one. What is the mass of these objects?	
Fran:	135 grams	
Teresa:	Thanks, Fran. How did you work that out so quickly?	
Fran:	I knew that the intervals were in five grams. Half way between 100 and 150 is 125, so I counted on from there.	
Teresa:	Let's all do that together. So tell us again how you knew that this was 125 grams? (*Places the red marker on the scale.*)	
Fran:	It is half way between the 100 grams and the 150 grams. So it must be 125 grams.	
Teresa:	Good. And then?	
Fran:	There are five grams in each interval.	
Teresa:	How do you know that?	
Fran:	It is written up there! (*Points to the interval tool on the screen. General laughter around the class.*)	
Teresa:	Yes, well done clever clogs! If you didn't have that to help, what could you do?	
Fran:	Well there are ten marks between the zero and the fifty, so that's five grams.	
Teresa:	Well done. Let's count those together. (*Points to each interval as the class chant.*)	
All:	5, 10, 15, 20, 25, 30, 35, 40, 45, 50, 55, 60, 65, 70, 75, 80, 85, 90, 95, 100.	
Teresa:	Right. So we know that these intervals represent five grams each. You knew that this was 125 grams, so what did you do?	
Fran:	I counted around ten more.	
Teresa:	Let's all do that. 125 –	
All:	130, 135.	
Teresa:	Good. Let's check. (*Clicks the 'show total' button.*) Well done! You were right. Who would like to come and select the next mass?	

Extending subject knowledge

Chapter 4 also considers how to vary level of content for a range of attainment levels.

Using questioning and resources to support children to read scales

Teresa's questioning techniques were every similar with both classes, yet she pitched the content of the questions at an appropriate level for the children she was working with each time. She was focused on the children being able to read the scale (on the scales!) accurately and with confidence. In doing so, she asked them to explain how they worked out the answer. With the Year 2 children this involved them explaining the different methods they used such as counting on and counting back from a known number. The Year 5 children were given the opportunity to do this also but Teresa also focused on how the children might work out what the intervals on the scale were.

Using whole-class demonstration resources such as the interactive teaching programme (ITP) has certain advantages. For example, the scale on the ITP was large enough for all the children to see. This saved Teresa some time in demonstrating to the children, as it could be done to the class together, although teaching to the whole class might not be as effective as working with smaller focus groups. Teresa used some of the capabilities of the ITP such as the 'show total' option and the red pointer that counted each interval to support the children while they were explaining their answers. Another of the advantages of this ITP is that it does not show the units that are being measured. This meant that Teresa was able to refer to appropriate units for the items: kilograms with the Year 2 pupils and grams with the Year 5 pupils.

While the ITP and similar ICT resources provide advantages such as those outlined above, it is important to be aware of the limitations present when using these types of resources. There are some skills required for reading a scale that using the ITP cannot replicate. One of these is the need to ensure that the eye line is at the same height as the scale being read. By reading a scale from above, below or the side it is possible to 'read' a result that is quite some way 'off the mark'. Some children will benefit from being able to touch the scale themselves, to help them make sense of the measurement. It is not possible to do this with an ITP, although in this case study the ITP provides one marker which goes some way to meeting that need, albeit the teacher is in control of it. Additionally, the children were not handling weights and using a set of scales themselves. This meant that they were not given the opportunity to develop their understanding about the mass being discussed, although this was not the objective of the starter.

Using appropriate terminology with pupils: mass or weight?

It is clear that there is much confusion for children and teachers over which terminology to use when working with mass and weight (Mullet and Gervais, 1990).

Galili (2001) presents a very interesting discussion about the historical development of weight vs. gravitational force and the implications for teaching children these difficult concepts. He suggests that children will have a greater understanding of these concepts if a distinction was made between weight and gravitational force, and that weight (as the measurement of gravitational force) was replaced by an operational definition. He offers three such definitions: that weight is

(a) the force exerted on a support by an *object*;
(b) the force exerted on an object by a *support*; and
(c) the force exerted on an object causing its spontaneous fall with acceleration.

If the support is a scale in (a) or (b), then the weight can be measured (Galili, 2001, p1083) in units such as kilograms or ounces.

3. Relationships between km, m and cm; kg and g; l and ml

Using the correct unit of measure is useful for a number of reasons. First, it enables the most effective way to record information. For example, it is ludicrous to say that a grain of rice is approximately 0.004m long when it is possible to use millimetres, or that I have the equivalent of 462.2 10-pence pieces in my purse, when I have £46.22. Second, it helps children to be able to select the most appropriate tool to undertake the measuring with. For example, measuring the length of a seedling in a science experiment is best done with a ruler with millimetres. Third, we utilise our strategies of estimation and approximation when we decide what unit to use and also when we use the units.

You can read more about the need for precise measurements in Chapter 3.

You can read more about the relationships between numbers in Chapter 2.

Being able to convert between metric units of the same attribute (for example, km to m to cm to mm in length) successfully is based upon a good knowledge and understanding of our place value system.

CASE STUDY: CONVERTING WITH MEANING AND UNDERSTANDING (YEAR 4)

Context
In this case study, the class have been given a week to demonstrate that the statements on a list provided by their teacher, Janet, are accurate. They have been provided with a vast array of resources to choose from. Each day the lesson is structured so that first, each group chooses a statement they are going to explore; second, they have collaborative group work time to prove the statement; and third, the groups present their findings to the rest of the class. Any statement that has been previously proved can be attempted again in a different way by any other group. We join the class during the plenary on the third day.

Curriculum Content
National Curriculum Key Stage 2
Pupils should be taught to:

Ma3.4a: recognise the need for standard units of length, mass and capacity, choose which ones are suitable for a task, and use them to make sensible estimates in everyday situations; convert one metric unit to another...

Primary Framework Year 4
Choose and use standard metric units and their abbreviations when

---

estimating, measuring and recording length, weight and capacity; know the meaning of 'kilo', 'centi' and 'milli' ...

Task

How does manipulating the water and the various measuring tools help the children to develop a deeper understanding of capacity?

Capacity statement sheet

How many of these can your group prove are correct?

1. There are 1,000ml in a litre
2. 15ml = 1 tablespoon
3. A decilitre is one tenth of a litre
4. A cup (used for baking) holds ¼ of a litre
5. A millilitre is 1/1000th of a litre
6. A teaspoon is 5ml
7. Half a litre is 500ml
8. One tablespoon is equivalent to three teaspoons
9. There are 2.5ml in half a teaspoon
10. One litre of water fits into a cube with sides 10cm long

Janet: James, Helen, Georgia and Michael. Which statement did you prove today?

Georgia: We did number 7. Half a litre is 500ml.

Janet: Thank you. Before we hear your method, which other groups have already demonstrated that statement? (Several hands go up.) Thank you. Let's see if you can demonstrate that half a litre is 500ml in a different way to these two groups.

Michael: First, we took this jug that had 500 ml on it and we filled it up to there. (*Points to the 500ml. James fills the jug with 500ml of water.*) Then we poured it in to the litre jug. We thought that it was about half way.

James: Then we did it again (*fills the 500ml jug*) and poured that in too. That showed us that there two lots of 500ml in a litre, which is 1,000ml. And half of 1,000 is 500 and half of a litre is what is in this jug which is 500ml.

Janet: Thank you. Does anyone want to ask any questions?

Laura: How do you know that the measurements on the jugs are right?

Janet: That happened to your group, didn't it Laura? You used a jug that you thought was a litre, but it wasn't quite, was it?

James: Well, these have marks on them all the way up the, um ...

Janet: Scale.

James: Scale, yeah. And so they should be right.

Georgia: But then we did something else after.

Janet: Oh! What was that, Georgia?

Georgia: We took this beaker here, that says that there are 100ml in it, see? (*Points to the 100ml scale.*) And we found that there were ten of those in the litre. So half of that is five and five lots of 100ml are 500ml. So we showed it that way too.

Extending subject knowledge

Using experiments to develop and demonstrate children's understanding of measures

Janet used a range of effective teaching methods to help the children further their knowledge and understanding of capacity conversions.

First, she presented them with the key ideas she wanted them to know by the end of the unit (for example, 1,000 millilitres is equivalent to 1 litre) as well as others that she thought they would find interesting and that may help them to demonstrate others. By presenting the children with the facts and asking them to prove them, the children were discussing the reasons behind why the statements were true and this constantly reinforced the conversions Janet wanted them to learn.

Second, the approach Janet used encouraged her pupils to develop not only their knowledge of the set conversions, but also, importantly, their understanding of how heavy a litre felt and what a litre (and all the various fractions of a litre) looked like in a range of vessels. This provided the children with a far deeper understanding of capacity that work without the water and the other resources would have.

Third, the children were encouraged to consider different ways that the same statements could be demonstrated. They were not allowed (due to the number of statements and the number of days this was carried out) to accept the first response a group gave. Through this they learned that there were many valid ways to work through the same problems and that everyone's ideas were valued. Pragmatically, it also allowed groups who 'wanted to do that one' a chance to work through it during the unit.

Finally, through all the methods discussed above, Janet gave her pupils the opportunity to reflect on their own learning and share ownership of their learning.

> **FURTHER READING**
> Global Footprints is a project from the Humanities Education Centre in Tower Hamlets, London. Go to www.globalfootprints. org/teachers/matrix.htm for lesson ideas on water.

> **REMINDER**
> Colour water with a food colouring or art dye so that it is easier for children to read scales and demonstrate to others.

4. Estimating length

In Chapter 3 there is some discussion on estimation and rounding in a numerical context. However, for all the same reasons, estimation is an important skill in all areas of mathematics. Through work on the Family Mathematics Project, Onslow (2002, cited in Sauer, 2002) wrote: *The skill (of estimation) is developed through practice and reflection. The more we do it, and the more we think about why we do it, the better we become. To be successful children need many opportunities to practise estimation and to learn from previous experiences.*

CASE STUDY: WHEN THE DINOSAURS ROAMED (YEAR 4)

Context
In this case study, Alan has designed sets of cards with ice lolly sticks attached that each show a picture of a dinosaur and its length in metres. The class has gone out to the field in groups and are setting out the cards according to their estimates of the length of the dinosaurs. When all groups

are finished, they will use the long tape measures to check the accuracy of their estimates.

Curriculum Content

<u>National Curriculum Key Stage 2</u>
Pupils should be taught to:

Ma3.4a: recognise the need for standard units of length, mass and capacity, choose which ones are suitable for a task, and use them to make sensible estimates in everyday situations; convert one metric unit to another...

<u>Primary Framework Year 4</u>
Choose and use standard metric units and their abbreviations when estimating and recording length ... and where appropriate use decimal notation.

Task

What opportunities does working outside the classroom afford these pupils in this case study?

Joe:	Right. Put all the cards in order and then we can start with the shortest one and go to the longest one.
Sajid:	Yeah, spread them out. OK. Oviraptor. That is the shortest. 1.5 metres.
Keith:	Velociraptor is next. 1.8.
Joe:	OK, so they are only, um, point 3 apart. What is that?
Sajid:	30 centimetres.
Joe:	Oh yeah.
William:	The triceratops is 7.9. Is that the next one?
Keith:	Yeah. We'll do those two short ones first and then we'll go to 7.9 metres.
Sajid:	Well, my dad said that my step, if I stretch, is about one metre. So (*steps one stride*) that is about a metre.
Joe:	And go half again.
Keith:	Well that is about half of that. (*Shows a spanned distance with his two forearms placed on the ground.*).
Sajid:	OK. That's good. Put it in. Which one is it? Oviraptor. 1.5 metres.
Joe:	Velociraptor is 30 centimetres more. That's a ruler. Did anyone bring out a ruler?
William:	No, we weren't allowed. But it is about that, isn't it? (*Shows a distance between his two hands.*)
Keith:	I think it is a bit smaller than that. (*Holds his hands near William's to compare.*) What do you think?
Joe:	Huh?
Keith:	Which one?
Joe:	Dunno. Saj – what do you think?
Sajid:	Oh definitely that one. (*Points to Keith's hands.*)
Keith:	(*Moves to put his hands on the grass.*) There. (*Points to the position for the next card. Card is placed in the grass.*) Right. Now what?
William:	Triceratops. It is 7.9 metres long.
Keith:	So where are we now?

Sajid:	1.8 metres.
Joe:	So we want to go another six metres.
William:	And a bit.
Joe:	Well, yeah. Saj, go six steps from here. That is ten centimetres from there.

Extending subject knowledge

Mathematics outside the classroom

The Early Years Foundation Stage (DfES, 2007b) now requires that an outdoor play area must be set up as part of children's access to continuous provision. Based on research into how young children learn, the guidance materials for the EYFS outline why outdoor play is important in Early Years settings. Arguably all of these apply to working with children of an older age, but for this case study it is clear that the children were benefiting from their outside activity because it:

FURTHER READING
To learn more about using the environment as a mathematical resource, read Chapter 7 by Cunningham in Drews and Hansen (eds), *Using resources to support mathematical thinking*. Exeter: Learning Matters.

- provided opportunities for developing harmonious relationships with others, through negotiation, taking turns and co-operation;
- supported those children who learn best through activity or movement;
- supported children's developing creativity and problem-solving skills. (DfES, 2007, pp1–2)

Estimations: a reasonable guess

In order to estimate the dinosaurs' lengths, the children were making comparisons with known lengths (such as a 30cm ruler) and their previous knowledge ('my dad says …'). These mental resources helped the children to estimate with reason.

Once the children had completed their first estimations, Alan instructed the groups to check their first three estimates with a 50m tape measure. On completion of this task, the children were given time to amend their estimates in light of the feedback they had just received from their measurements. Because of the perceived competitive element within this task, some complained that it was 'cheating'. However, Alan observed a very positive effect of including this intermediate step. By having an opportunity to respond to the feedback, the children proactively amended their estimations, using a wealth of numerical and measurement vocabulary and applying their new-found knowledge alongside their existing knowledge for a second time. This additional focused discussion in groups would have never happened if the children had been allowed to run the tape measure against all their first estimations and simply check them off.

Alan concluded the lesson with a class discussion on the various techniques and mental models the children used to support their estimations. They considered how these techniques varied according to the lengths. They also found that the shorter the length, the more confident the children were in estimating it.

5. Perimeter and area

Perimeter and area are notoriously difficult for children to distinguish between (Barrett and Clemson, 1998). However, with appropriate instruction it is possible to help children to develop their understanding. For example, Cass et al. (2003) worked with children who had been diagnosed with learning disabilities in mathematics over a two-month period. They found that using manipulatives along-side modelling as well as guided practice and independent practice developed the pupils' problem-solving skills, and that they were able to transfer these to pencil-and-paper problems effectively.

CASE STUDY: PERIMETER AND AREA (YEAR 6)

Context
In this case study, the pupils have been set the following task: 'Draw as many shapes as you can with a perimeter of 24cm. Calculate the area of each shape. Which shape has the largest area? Why?'

Curriculum Content
National Curriculum Key Stage 2
Pupils should be taught to:

Ma3.4e: find perimeters of simple shapes; find areas or rectangles using the formula, understanding its connection to counting squares and how it extends its approach; calculate the perimeter and area of shapes composed of rectangles.

Primary Framework Year 6
Calculate the perimeter and area of rectilinear shapes; estimate the area of an irregular shape by counting squares.

Task
Why does the area of various shapes, all with the same length of perimeter, change even though the perimeter remains constant? How might you explain this to children?

Tom's work in finding shapes with a perimeter of 24 cm:

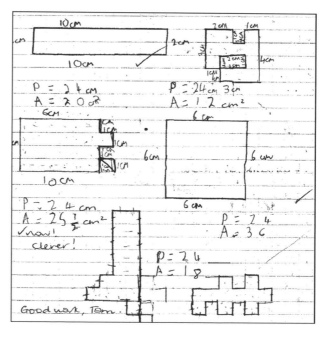

Extending subject knowledge

Calculating area and counting area

In the work above, Tom has demonstrated his understanding of perimeter and area. He has challenged himself to create a range of shapes with a perimeter of 24cm, as asked, and he has identified that the shape with the largest area is the square, at 36cm^2. It is interesting to note from his work that it appears he has calculated the area of the rectangle and the square by calculation, probably area = length × width because the paper inside those shapes is clean. There are clear marks on his work where he has counted the squares to find the area of the other shapes. The teacher has noted this, and she is going to work with Tom to encourage him to use his knowledge of calculating the area of rectilinear shapes alongside counting, so that the area of a shape such as the one in the centre at the bottom can be worked out using a combination of the two strategies. She is also going to remind Tom about including the units (in this case cm^2) each time.

FURTHER READING
To read more about how to calculate the area of 2-D shapes, read pages 84-8 of Mooney et al. (2007) *Primary mathematics: knowledge and practice.* Exeter: Learning Matters.

How could this task be taken further?

Is the area of the square that Tom found the greatest that can be made? One quick way to visually demonstrate this is to knot a length of string that is 24cm long. By some easy manipulation, it is possible to show the idea that a circle might be the shape that produces the largest area.

Another method might be to calculate the areas of some regular polygons and draw conclusions from the data. These calculations – shown in the table below – were carried out using The Regular Polygons Calculator at www.cleavebooks. co.uk/scol/calpolyg.htm. There are a number of similar pages and java applets that enable you to quickly undertake these calculations. These could be used on an interactive whiteboard with a class.

No. of sides	Length of sides (cm)	Area	No. of sides	Length of sides (cm)	Area
3	8	27.7cm^2	8	3	43.5cm^2
4	6	36cm^2	9	2.67	44cm^2
5	4.8	39.6cm^2	10	2.4	44.3cm^2
6	4	41.6cm^2	11	2.18	44.5cm^2
7	3.43	42.7cm^2	12	45.8	44.8cm^2

By looking at what happens to the area as the shape becomes closer and closer to a circle, it is possible to generalise that the circle would have the largest area.
So what is the area of the circle? We know that to calculate the area of a circle, we use πr^2.

The circumference is calculated using πd. So $d = c/\pi$.

The circumference of our circle is 24cm: 24 / 3.147 = 7.626. So the diameter is 7.626cm.

REMINDER
This calculation was undertaken by numbers that were rounded to three decimal places. A more accurate answer would be 45.837.

We need to halve that to find the radius. The radius is 3.813cm.

So $\pi d \ r^2 = \pi \ (3.813)^2 = 45.754cm^2$.

And that is the largest area we can find!

7
Handling data

Introduction

It is quite fitting that handling data sits within the final chapter of this book because it enables people to bring many other aspects of mathematics together to help them make sense of the world. For example, processing, presenting and interpreting data is paramount to being able to reason and communicate about mathematics and solve problems. The obvious relationship between number and handling data is reflected in the National Curriculum where processing, representing and interpreting data is subsumed in Key Stage 1 within the Number Programme of Study (DfES, 1999, p64), although handling data becomes a separate Programme of Study in Key Stage 2 (Ma4).

In this chapter we will look at five aspects of handling data:

1. *Sorting.* Why do young children sort spontaneously and intuitively? What are the benefits of role play? At what age should role play be used to support mathematical learning? This section includes an Early Years Foundation Stage case study about a Reception child in a role as a post-man.

2. *Representing data.* Why do we need to create and use representations of data? What are the stages of the data handling process? What are the benefits of working in a group to represent data? Why is encouraging children to analyse representations of data essential? This section includes a Year 1 case study about children representing data in a pictogram.

3. *Designing questions.* What questions could be used to stimulate children about their work on handing data? What are the possible avenues of investigation from these questions? Why is starting from the children's interests beneficial? This section includes a short report on the interests of a few children aged 5 to 11.

4. *Purpose and audience in processing, presenting and interpreting data.* Why should children feel a sense of ownership in their work? What is the purpose of providing a wider audience for children's work? This section includes a Year 4 case study about two pupils who talk about their data handling in their group research projects.

5. *Measures of average.* What are the mean, median, mode and range? How are these used and why do we need different measures of average? What contexts might be used to introduce measures of average to children? This section includes a Year 6 case study about a group of children helping the teacher plan for her holiday.

FURTHER READING
Drews (2007) discusses
sorting further in
Chapter 3 in Drews and
Hansen (eds) *Using
resources to support
mathematical thinking.*
Exeter: Learning
Matters.

1. Sorting

Sorting is one of the most fundamental aspects of mathematics because it helps young children begin to make sense of their world. It is something that they undertake spontaneously and intuitively from a young age (Reys et al., 1995). The skills that children learn when sorting and classifying are many and varied. For example, sorting and classifying help children to understand the notion of belonging to a group and also to understand that objects can be grouped or regrouped in a range of ways (Platz, 2004), both aspects of reasoning and logic. For example, a blue circle could be grouped with the circles, the blue shapes or in a set of blue circles. Additionally, the number six could be grouped with even numbers, multiples of 2, multiples of 3, multiples of 2 and 3 or factors of 24, for example.

CASE STUDY: THE POSTMAN (EYFS)

Context
In this case study, the teaching assistant, Danni, is working with a group of Reception children who are in the role play area. The children have recently visited the local Post Office and they have designed their role play area from this visit.

Curriculum Content
The Early Learning Goals
Problem Solving, Reasoning and Numeracy: Sort familiar objects to identify their similarities and differences.

Task
What is the value of role play in supporting children's mathematical development?

Danni:	What are you doing here, Ellie?
Ellie:	I am the postman.
Danni:	Hello postman. What are you doing?
Ellie:	I am sorting my parcels out.
Danni:	Oh, I see. How are you doing that?
Ellie:	The big parcels go in there and the small parcels go in there.
Danni:	Will you have enough room in those bags for all those parcels?
Ellie:	I got a big one for the big parcels and a small one for the small parcels.
Danni:	When you have sorted them, what are you going to do?
Ellie:	I am going to deliver them to the houses. (*Points to the 'houses', which are boxes numbered and colour coded for the parcels to be delivered to.*)
Danni:	You are going to have a busy morning, postman.
Ellie:	Yes. (*Stands up and carries bags to the 'houses'.*) One big one for the yellow house. Number 5. (*Puts the large yellow box with a number 5 on it in the yellow box numbered 5.*) One big one for Mr Blue. That's your birthday present. What number is that?
Danni:	That is number two.
Ellie:	Two. Blue. Haha! (*Laughs, then chants.*) Two for blue, two for blue ... (*Continues placing the parcels into the boxes, reciting the*

colour names or the numbers, or asking for the number names.)

Danni: Have you finished delivering all the parcels now?

Ellie: Yes, none of them got letters. They all got parcels. And presents and things.

Danni: How many did the orange house get?

Ellie: It got three. Three parcels for the orange house. I'm the postman and I took them. One, two, three. Look.

Danni: Yes, I can see those. You delivered them well, postman!

Extending subject knowledge

Role play

Role play offers opportunity for children to put themselves in someone else's shoes. Wood (2007, p119) refers to young children as *competent social actors within a complex network of social and cultural influences* and role play enables children to try out ideas they have in a safe, supportive environment, trying out mathematical (and of course other!) ideas.

FURTHER READING
The ATM (2003) have produced a book called *Young children learning mathematics* in which a number of articles discuss role play and other interesting areas of developing mathematics with 3–7 year old children.

Ellie had chosen to classify the parcels into 'big' and 'small' parcels, and had chosen bags representative of those sets. Later, she sorted according to colour and made attempts to match and say the names of the numbers on the parcels. The teaching assistant was able to help Ellie to say the number names out loud and ask questions about the way she is sorting the letters. The notion of sorting according to size, colour and number was considered and the opportunity for the children to explore these was intentionally designed during the planning of this role play area.

The children's participation during the conception and creation of the role play area is particularly interesting. In this school, the role play areas are numerous and varied, and they are always based on the children's personal experiences or class trips. This Post Office was no different. In order to plan the role play area, the children scrutinised photographs from their trip. They wrote, with the help of the teacher and the teaching assistants, what they wanted to have in their own Post Office and they planned it together. Many of the artefacts were brought in from children's homes (through a request in the class weekly newsletter home to parents) and the children took an active part in creating all the things in the Post Office such as the sorting room and the Post Office counter, including tax discs etc.! This had the positive effect of the children feeling ownership of the role play area. They often approached the school staff with ideas for new role play areas, and these were usually taken forward. Involving the children at that stage ensured a smooth transition from the visit to the role play. During the planning and creating of the role play area, there were additional opportunities for the children to use and apply their mathematical skills, knowledge and understanding with purpose.

Role play should not be limited to the Early Years Foundation Stage and Key Stage 1 children. Play is central to Key Stage 2 children's lives also. Wallace (2005), for example, explains how computer technology supports middle-school children in their mathematical development. Wallace discusses a number of issues that designing and using computer technology raises and these are similar to traditional role play areas. These include the balance of freedom of action and structured learning sequence, motivation and rewards, academic progress, higher-order thinking skills and flexible learning and teaching strategies. Another example of role play in Key Stage 2 is provided by Eyles (1999) where Years 5 and 6 children were 'paid' to come to school for a two-week cross-curricular unit of work incorporating money. During that time they became members of a community who paid tax on their income, paid rent on their tables and chairs, banked their money and earned interest, and set up their own enterprise businesses.

2. Re-presenting data

We re-present data to make it possible to gather the information we require efficiently and effectively. For example, this book contains a contents page and indexes so that the information it contains can be found more easily than looking at every page within it. How data is represented depends on what question is being asked. Data may be represented with iconic representations (as in a pictogram), displaying proportions of data (as in a pie chart) or showing a trend over time (as in a line graph). It may also be represented using measures of averages (see later in this chapter).

It is not uncommon for data to be displayed in misleading ways in order to influence people in a particular way, perhaps for political spin. It is possible to find misleading graphs and tables in the media on a regular basis. Children should be taught the ways in which to display data accurately using mathematical conventions. This will help them to present their data without unintentionally misleading an audience.

Rodrigues (1994) found that most children believe that a graph is something to present at the end point of some research. However, it is important to remember that there is a research cycle which children (and teachers) can dip into and out of as appropriate. This involves: posing a question, thinking about what data is required to answer the question, planning how to gather and record the data (is it primary or secondary data that is required?); analysing the data (does it answer my question?); presenting the data; and, most importantly, discussing the data.

CASE STUDY: EYE COLOUR (YEAR 1)

Context
In this case study, the children have become rather interested in eye colour, so the teacher, Pauline, has decided to use this as the context to introduce pictograms.

Curriculum Content
National Curriculum Key Stage 1
Pupils should be taught to:

Ma2.5a: solve a relevant problem by using simple lists, tables and charts to sort, classify and organise information.

Ma2.5b: discuss what they have done and explain their results.

Primary Framework Year 1
Answer a question by recording information in lists and tables; present outcomes using practical resources, pictures, block graphs or pictograms. Use diagrams to sort objects into groups according to a given criterion; suggest a different criterion for grouping the same objects.

Task
What is the value of children using information about themselves when they are starting to learn how data can be presented?

The children have been given a card with an eye drawn on it and they have been asked to colour it in the same colour as their own eye:

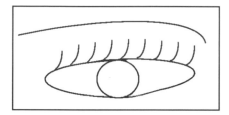

Pauline: Can you please all come down onto the carpet again, with your coloured eye? (*All children come and sit facing the board.*) Who can remind us what we have been doing at our tables?

Ahmed: We have been colouring our eyes.

Pauline: That is right, Ahmed. You have all been colouring the pupils on the cards I gave you the same colour as your own eyes. Good. Why have we been doing that?

Ahmed: Because we want to find out how many different colours there are and which one has the most.

Pauline: Yes. Well explained. So let's find out which colours we have in the classroom using a pictogram. What colour is your eye, Tasha?

Tasha: It is brown.

Pauline: Can you please bring your eye up to the board? (*Pauline takes Tasha's eye and sticks it onto the board.*) Who else has a brown eye? (*13 children put their hands up.*) That is a lot of people! I would like you to bring your eyes up one at a time so we can stick your cards to the board too, above Tasha's. (*This forms a column of brown eyes on the board.*) What other coloured eyes do we have in the class? Holly, what colour are your eyes?

Holly: Hazel.

Pauline: Does anyone else have hazel-coloured eyes? (*No one responds.*) Holly! You are the only person in the class with hazel eyes. That makes you rather special! Come and put your card up. (*This goes on the board next to the brown eyes, forming a new 'column' of one.*) Does anyone have blue eyes? (*Several children put their hands up. This is continued until the class have produced their own pictogram.*)

The colour of eyes in our class

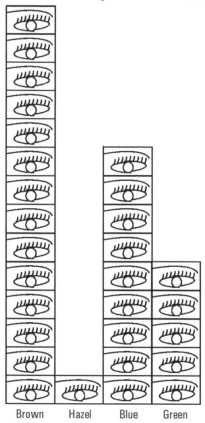

| Brown | Hazel | Blue | Green |

Pauline:	Now that we have created our pictogram, who can tell me which colour is the most popular eye colour in this class?
Tasha:	It is brown.
Pauline:	Yes, Tasha. Well done. How many of you have brown eyes? Let's count together. (*Pauline counts from the bottom of the brown column upwards, leading the counting.*)
All:	1, 2, 3, … 12, 13, 14.
Pauline:	So there are how many people in the class with brown eyes?
All:	Fourteen.
Pauline:	Well done. Brown is the most popular eye colour. Which is the next most popular eye colour?
Tina:	Blue.
Pauline:	How did you know that?
Tina:	It is the next highest tower.
Pauline:	Very good, Tina. You didn't have to count them, did you? You could tell that blue was the second most popular colour by seeing that it was the next tallest column. Well done. I have a tricky question for you all now. How many more people in the classroom have blue eyes than have green eyes? (*Repeats question, pointing to the blue and green columns on the pictogram.*)
Aaron:	Four more.

Pauline:	Can you come and show us how you worked that out, Aaron?
Aaron:	(*Pointing to the four blue eyes above the green column.*) One, two, three, four.
Pauline:	That's brilliant, Aaron! So you knew there were that many green eyes (*motions to the five green eye cards*) and then there were (*keeps counting*) one, two, three, four more blue eyes. Did you have to count how many green eyes there were?
Aaron:	No.
Pauline:	No, you could count from there, to the top of the blue eyes column. Well done, Aaron.

Extending subject knowledge

Developing a graph collaboratively

By creating the pictograph as a class, Pauline was able to help the children to develop some important aspects of data representation. First, they all knew that their own personal information became one part within the class graph. This is an important notion to understand so that when more abstract forms of data representation are used later, children understand that the charts are still representing members of a set. Second, Pauline was able to model some of the conventions for creating a graph: there was a title; the units were represented uniformly and the x-axis was even along the horizontal axis. Finally, Pauline used the graph effectively. For example, when counting with the children, Pauline started at the base of the brown eyes column and counted up. This modelled the way that the children should be reading the bars and the scales. It would also have been plausible for the children to stand in a place in the classroom or playground to make a 'human graph'.

> **REMINDER**
> Some children might be sensitive about being the only child in the class to have a particular attribute. This is particularly the case with height and weight. Be sensitive to children's responses and amend your plans if necessary.

Using a graph to analyse the data

By using the graph to analyse the data represented by the children, Pauline was demonstrating why graphs and charts are produced. Many teachers draw their lesson or unit of work to a close once the children have produced their graphs (Rodrigues, 1994). If this happens, the pupils are not being given the opportunity to understand why charts are produced, and they see graphs as the product or end-point, rather than the tool to answer a question or solve a problem. As mentioned above, charts are used to enable people to make sense of data more easily because they present the data in a more ordered and clearer way to scrutinise. They are a tool within the cycle of handling data. The data collection and representation is only a part of the cycle, and is a means to an end, not an end in itself.

> **REMINDER**
> 'Data' is plural, so you would say, 'the data are well presented'.

Pauline worked with the children to help them make sense of the data that was represented. They were all keen because it was a topic about them personally and the topic had been chosen by Pauline because eye colour had come up in casual conversations between the children and had captured their imaginations. Tina generalised the information on the pictogram and used it well. She referred to the length of the columns rather than counting the pictures. This was reinforced by Pauline because it is a skill that she wanted all the pupils to develop eventually. The other skill that Pauline spent some time building upon was Aaron's counting on strategy for working out the difference between the number of children with blue

Read more about counting on in Chapter 4.

and green eyes. He also used Tina's strategy of taking the columns as wholes, and he counted *from* the top of the green column *to* the top of the blue column in order to calculate the difference.

3. Designing questions

This section has been included to encourage you to think about the wide range of questions you might encourage your children to answer during their work in school. There is a place for the 'colour of eyes' type projects outlined in the case study above, but it is also essential to note that there are (probably!) an infinite number of avenues where handling data can be utilised and exploited.

It is worthwhile considering the topics being learnt in other curriculum areas. For example, it might be useful to access the local census information gathered since 1801, or historical maps of the local area to answer questions on how the area has developed over time. This type of investigation is highly effective because it involves complex interpretation skills by the children as opposed to the rather narrow interpretation required by questions such as 'what is your favourite pop band?' It also brings to the children a deeper knowledge and understanding about the purposes for which data are recorded and how data can be used powerfully to answer probing questions about us, our location or history.

CASE STUDY: WHAT INTERESTS YOU? (ALL AGES)

Context
In this case study, I share what I found out when I asked 70 children (ten from each year group from Reception to Year 6) what they were interested in finding out about.

Curriculum Content
National Curriculum Key Stage 2
Pupils should be taught to:

Ma4.2a: solve problems involving data.

Primary Framework Years 1–4
Answer a question...

Year 5: Answer a set of questions ...

Year 6: Solve problems by collecting, selecting, processing and interpreting data, using ICT where appropriate; draw conclusions and identify further questions to ask.

Task
What other cross-curricular questions might you encourage pupils to ask?

The following is a list of only two of the responses I received from the ten children in each year group I questioned. They show a level of insight and inquisitiveness that is worth harnessing.

Children's responses	Possible avenues of research in response
Reception	
Why does my telly go to sleep at seven o'clock?	Favourite television programme (check everyone has a TV first). Television characters (*why* do you like …?)
How many steps is it to school?	How do we get to school? How long does it take to get to school?
Year 1	
Why can't you keep a tarantula as a pet? What do pets eat?	A visit to the pet shop.
Why does the grass grow at night?[1]	Watching seeds grow. Which is the fastest/tallest/etc.
Year 2	
Why do I have to eat my vegetables?	Least popular vegetables (pass information to the school canteen). Find out why vegetables are healthy. Link to adjectives in English.
Why does it always rain when we are going somewhere special?	Noting the weather. Does it really rain when it is a special day, or do you just notice it more?
Year 3	
Why do you only have one birthday in a year?	Popular toys: asking toy shops about their best-selling toys. Compare with our class. Birthdays in the class.
Is there a school trip this year? Where would the children in the class like to go?	Relate to the upcoming topics. Visiting speakers to the class: who would interest you? Why?
Year 4	
Which is the best mobile phone?	Research prices of calls/texts/tariffs/etc.
Who is going to win the league this year?	Rather than favourite team (boring!), look at highest-paid players, most red cards, number of team coaches employed over the past x years, distance travelled to away matches …
Year 5	
Why do we have to pay so much in the canteen for crisps?	Survey of food likes/dislikes. Preferred costs of items. Present to the cook and head teacher.
What is the cost of a funeral?[2]	What is required for a funeral? Costing the items Modelling the cost. Compare Egyptian funeral with modern-day funeral.
Year 6	
What is the longest book anyone has ever read?	How many pages do books have? Is there a reason for that number of pages? Compare most popular books with number of pages: is there a relationship? (Use a scattergraph.)
How much money is owed to our country by other countries?	How will we get it back? World debt. Credit card debt. Interests on credit cards. Mortgage rates.

1. My response was, 'Why do you think it grows at night?', to which she replied, 'Well, I don't see it growing during the day'.
2. I include this as 'food for thought'. This is not the first time I have met a child with an interest in this area. A Year 6 child I taught wanted to learn more about human embalming. With their parents' permission, a small group of his friends had a tour of a mortuary. They wrote about it in a mathematics project. A note of caution: this is a potentially sensitive area that must be handled carefully.

Using the children's interests and to██████████ork as starting points

My point in sharing the above table with you is to highlight the vast range of topics that can be explored through the children's interests and also within the topics that you are planning to study with them. The Early Years Foundation Stage (DfES, 2007c) and the Every Child Matters Agenda (DfES, 2004) both have central tenets regarding the child being at the centre of our provision. By building on the interests of the pupils we teach, we are developing a more personalised learning approach. Research (e.g. Rudduck and Flutter, 2004) shows that when children felt that they were being listened to, they felt that they were being taken more seriously as learners, they could manage their own progress more effectively and they felt more included in the classroom and school community.

4. Purpose and audience in processing, presenting and interpreting data

This section builds on the previous as it considers purpose and audience in handling data. Children are likely to learn more effectively if they see a purpose for their work (Ainley et al., 2006).

CASE STUDY: A DATA-HANDLING PROJECT (YEAR 4)

Context
In this case study, the class were allowed to work in self-selected groups to choose a topic for a week-long project handling data. This case study reports the responses from two pupils, from two different groups, being questioned by an interviewer (I) to see what they learned.

Curriculum Content
National Curriculum Key Stage 2
Pupils should be taught to:

Ma4.2a: solve problems involving data.

Primary Framework Year 4
Answer a question by identifying what data to collect; organise, present, analyse and interpret the data in tables, diagrams, tally charts, pictograms and bar charts, using ICT where appropriate.

Task
What is the value of encouraging children to plan and execute their own research project?

I: What was your topic?

Laura: We looked at how many people didn't use the pedestrian crossing when it was less than fifteen metres away from them.

Lawrence: We looked at the colours of cars.

I: Why did you choose that?

Laura: Some of us went to school that way and we thought that there were a lot of adults doing an unsafe thing.

Lawrence: We like cars and we wanted to see if Stephen was right, because he said that white was the most popular colour.

I: How did you plan your week?

Laura: We spent Monday constructing our plan. Then we collected our data on Tuesday and Wednesday. We made our poster on Thursday and we presented our work to the class on Friday.

Lawrence: We planned our timetable on Monday and then we did our data collection the next two days. We spent Thursday making our poster and writing our letter to the car factory and then we presented our work on the last day.

I: Your posters?

Laura: Yes. We made a group poster and we used it to share what we found out with the class. Ours didn't go on the class wall. It went in the window of the shop opposite the pedestrian crossing!

Lawrence: Our poster went on the wall in the classroom, but we also wrote a letter to the car factory in the neighbouring town.

I: What did you learn in the week?

Laura: Well, you have to work well together otherwise you get behind. We used tallies to record our data and then we made bar graphs. I learnt that a lot of adults jay walk – that's what they call it in America. It is illegal over there. I think it should be here too.

Lawrence: Stephen was right. We did clock more white cars going along the street. But when we sent our work to the car factory, he said that the most common colour is metalic silver at the moment. So we can't have had any new car drivers around our school when we were looking! They didn't have the latest models.

I: What was the best part?

Laura: Being able to talk to the class about our work and then having our work displayed in the shop window so that other people can see it. I hope that it helps reduce the number of jay walkers you know.

Lawrence: Our trip to the car factory. Because after we sent our project away to them, they wrote back and invited us to the car factory. We told them all about our project and they showed us how the cars were made. It was ace!

Extending subject knowledge

Feeling ownership of one's work

The children from these two groups were very positive about their experiences of handling data through this project. They had planned, implemented and presented a topic of their own choice. Davies et al. (2003) report on the CensusAtSchool Project. One of the key outcomes was that it integrated both data-handling skills with information and communication technologies to enhance teachers' continued professional development. This involved raising awareness among children and teachers for the need to collect, present and analyse data well.

The case study projects above expected the children to decide which methods of data collection, analysis and presentation they were going to use. They were required to make informed decisions about these things and had to justify these to the teacher, making sure every member of the group was confident in that method. It is apparent from the interviews above that the children also had opinions about their assertions and their findings. The teacher commented that when the children did not know what mathematical skill or strategy to use to solve a particular issue or problem, they found it out. In this case, the children were using the context and their mathematical thinking strategies to learn more about handling data. This is a departure from more traditional methods of teaching (and, according to Askew et al. (1997a) a less effective way of teaching) where content is taught and *then* it is applied.

You can read more about having a sense of audience in Chapter 5.

Having an audience for one's work

By sharing the project with an external audience not directly related to the school, the children felt a great sense of worth in their work and immense pride from being able to develop it. This was heightened for some pupils. Because their teacher was so impressed with their final work, she arranged for four of the groups to present their work to the Year 6 class, who were rather motivated by what they saw and asked their own teacher if they could do the same type of project.

Without exception, the children received some acknowledgement of their work from the places they sent their work to. These ranged from letters of interest, to stickers and booklets, invitations to visit shops/factories, CD-Roms, a mention of their work on the company website and one in the local newspaper.

5. Measures of average

In the everyday world, the term 'average' is used to mean standard, typical, regular, usual, common, ordinary. However, in mathematics the term refers to the mean, median, mode or range. Younger children tend to use the word at school to mean the former sense, but it is at Key Stage 2 that we expect pupils to be using the latter (Mokros and Russell, 1995). The transition from informal to formal use causes children difficulty and it is this that needs careful thinking through in order to help children understand the measures of average we use (Watson and Moritz, 2000; Watson, 2007).

Averages are used to help us make sense of numerical data in a different way to representing it on a graph. For example, it is sometimes useful to look at the range: what is the spread of the data? What does that tell me about the data? Other times it is useful to look at the mode: what is the most frequently occuring data? What does that tell me?

CASE STUDY: MY SUMMER HOLIDAYS (YEAR 6)

Context

In this case study, the teacher, Maggie, has announced that she is going to South Africa during the Christmas holiday period. She wants the children to help her to plan her trip and organise everything that she might need to do in preparation for the trip. Groups are tasked with different areas of her trip, such as flights, currency, best places to stay ('cost vs. comfort'), unmissable visits, etc. One group is looking at what she should pack in her bag. They have itemised the essentials such as sunblock and camera and are now focusing on the clothing she should pack.

Curriculum Content
National Curriculum Key Stage 2
Pupils should be taught to:

Ma4.2d: *know that mode is a measure of average and that range is a measure of spread, and to use both ideas to describe data sets.*

Primary Framework Year 6
Describe and interpret results and solutions to problems using the mode, range, median and mean.

Task
What is the value of reinforcing mathematical language with young children?

Maggie:	So what sorts of things do I need to pack for my clothes then, guys?
Shareef:	Loads of clothes for hot weather, 'cos it is hot over there.
Maggie:	So, do I pack very cool clothes because it is blindingly hot over there, or do I pack cool clothes that I'd wear here in summer because it is similar to the English summer?
Shareef:	It's way hotter over there, Miss.
Maggie:	How do you know?
Shareef:	Because you see it on the telly all the time. Its like desert and stuff over there.
Maggie:	I'm not feeling very confident at the moment about your recommendations, Shareef. I think I need some evidence about the temperatures there over Christmas before I can pack what you suggest.

The children use the internet to find out the data that their teacher requires. They print off the following table (BBC, 2008):

Cape Town, South Africa									
Month	Average sunlight (hours)	Temperature				Discomfort from heat and humidity	Relative humidity		Average precipitation (mm)	Wet days (+0.25 mm)
		Average		Record						
		Min.	Max.	Min.	Max.		a.m.	p.m.		
Jan	11	16	26	7	37	Moderate	72	54	15	3
Feb	10	16	26	5	38	Moderate	77	54	8	2
March	9	14	25	6	39	Moderate	85	57	18	3
April	8	12	22	3	39	–	90	60	48	6
May	6	9	19	–1	35	–	91	65	79	9
June	6	8	18	–2	29	–	91	64	84	9
July	6	7	17	–2	29	–	91	67	89	10
Aug	7	8	18	–1	32	–	90	65	66	9
Sept	8	9	18	1	34	–	87	62	43	7
Oct	9	11	21	1	32	–	79	58	31	5
Nov	10	13	23	4	34	–	74	56	18	3
Dec	11	14	24	5	38	Moderate	71	54	10	3

Maggie:	Tell me about what you have found here, then.
Lee:	Well, when you're going, in December and January, the average maximum temperature is between 24 and 26 degrees.
Maggie:	What does that mean, 'the average'?
Lee:	The average, you know (*pause*), well, it's just the average, ain't it.
Maggie:	Hmmm. I'm not sure I understand yet, Lee. Could anyone else have a go?
Harry:	Yeah, it's like what it is most of the time. Like there, it is 24 degrees in December and 26 degrees in January. But then it is 17 in July in winter. Wow, that's warm for winter.
Maggie:	I still don't know from what you're telling me how they got to the 24 degrees, or 26 or 17 though.
Jack:	Well it is like the middle of the temperatures. So some of them are hotter and some are colder but it is what it is like overall, like the middle.
Maggie:	OK, I think I am beginning to understand, but I want you to do something else for me. I know that it is going to be, on average, 24 to 26 degrees. But, look at the minimum and maximum temperatures. What is the range of those?
Lee:	Gee, it goes from 5 to 38!
Maggie:	Yes, Lee. So Shareef, it can get really hot there, but should I take only cool clothes?
Shareef:	No, Miss, 'cos 5 degrees is quite cold.
Maggie:	So now I know that I have to take some warmer clothes for the cold days, and some very cool clothes for the very hot days, and a mixture in between. But what proportion of clothes should I take?
Lee:	Huh?
Maggie:	Well, is it likely to be cold a lot of days, so I need lots of warm clothes, and then other days really hot, so I'd need lots of very cool clothes, and no middle of the road clothes, or what?
Shareef:	You'd need a few of everything.
Maggie:	Is that an evidence-based comment, or have you made that up again? (*Smiles.*)
Shareef:	Haha. I – made it up!
Maggie:	Well, my friend brought this around to me last night because she thought I might be interested in seeing what the temperatures were in Cape Town in December and January last year.

DECEMBER						
M	Tu	W	Th	F	Sa	Su
	20	24	26	25	29	27
27	25	29	28	27	22	20
31	29	28	27	27	26	26
28	24	20	29	28	20	21
25	27	26	30			

JANUARY						
M	Tu	W	Th	F	Sa	Su
				27	24	22
18	16	18	28	25	26	28
21	24	25	18	19	25	24
20	28	26	27	30	29	34
28	27	25	22	22	23	25

Jack:	Oh that's good.
Maggie:	Why?
Jack:	Cos you can see what happens in the month.
Maggie:	OK, I'll leave you with this and come back in a while to see if you have decided how many clothes I need of each type.

Maggie returns after some time to find the following on a large sheet of paper:

DECEMBER:
16, 18, 18, 18, 19, 20, 21, 22, 22, 22, 23, 24, 24, 24, 25, 25, 25, 25, 26, 26, 27, 27, 27, 28, 28, 28, 28, 28, 28, 30, 34
= 801 ÷ 31 = 25.9

JANUARY:
20, 20, 20, 20, 21, 23, 24, 24, 25, 25, 25, 26, 26, 26, 26, 27, 27, 27, 27, 27, 27, 28, 28, 28, 28, 29, 29, 29, 29, 30, 31
= 754 ÷ 31 = 24.3

Maggie:	This looks interesting.
Jack:	We've got it now!
Maggie:	Aha! Tell me more.
Lee:	This is good. We ordered all the temperatures for each month because we kept losing count when we were counting them all up.
Maggie:	Why did you want to count them all up?
Lee:	So we could find the range of temperatures. So last year you wouldn't have needed clothes for as hot and cold as we said before, but you better take them this year in case.
Maggie:	Aha. So what was the range last year?
Shareef:	It was between 16 and 34.
Maggie:	Good. Now what else have you been doing here, with these circles and squares?
Jack:	Well you wanted to know how many of each thing to take. And we learnt that there were lots of days where it was 28 and 27 degrees, so you should take more clothes for that sort of temperature.
Maggie:	So the most days of the same temperature in December were 28 degrees and the most days of the same temperature in January were 27 degrees?
Jack:	Yeah. We thought that was funny because the average temperatures are the other way around. January is hotter than December.
Maggie:	It is interesting. So you have found the modes for each month there. The mode for December was 28 and the mode for January was 27 degrees. OK. What about those squares?
Shareef:	We worked out what the middle temperature was in that list and put a square around it.
Maggie:	Why did you do that?
Shareef:	Well, when we did it we worked out that half of the temperatures that month were above that temperature and half were below it.
Maggie:	Aha. That is called the median. The median. And this calculation? (*Points to the division sentence below each list of temperatures.*)
Lee:	We were trying to work out how the BBC did their average. We worked out that they added them all up and then divided them

Maggie:	by the number of days in the month. Did you?
Lee:	Sort of! Well, Mrs Girven (*the teaching assistant*) helped us out! (*All laugh.*)
Maggie:	Haha. That's good. What did Mrs Girven call that type of average?
All:	The mean.

Extending subject knowledge

Introducing and developing concepts of average

Maggie used her mathematical subject knowledge and pedagogical knowledge effectively with these children to introduce them to the mean, median, mode and range. She did so through:

- presenting the pupils with a meaningful, purposeful context to work within and learn about the different measures of the average through it;
- thoughtful and well prepared additional resources if the pupils required them to work through the task;
- encouraging the pupils to make evidenced decisions based on the data;
- introducing unknown mathematical concepts through tasks.

Measures of average as a starting point for statistical understanding: the meaning of the mean

The children began to develop their own understanding of mean, median, mode and range though this case study. It is the first time that they have knowingly calculated these averages and have done so efficiently within the context of the problem they had been set.

Initially the pupils struggled with defining what the BBC meant as 'average'. For example, Jack referred to it twice as being something to do with the 'middle'. Children (and teachers!) often struggle to define these averages with meaning. It is very easy to repeat, for example, that the mean is the sum of all numbers in the set divided by the number in the set. But to understand what that mean actually represents takes time through a number of contextualised tasks.

Another context that could be suitable might include house prices in the area. 'I'm looking at buying a house in this area.' Here, the mean, median, mode and range are all useful. For example, the mean could be used to look at the value of the houses in the area over time: have they risen/reduced in price over the last decade? The mean could be skewed by a new estate of very expensive properties, so other measures of average might be more useful. For example, the median provides the half-way mark of the house prices: Am I looking in the top half or the bottom half of the market? The mode is again useful: What is the most common house price in this area? What do I get for that money? Finally, the range: If I wanted to live in this area, how much could I spend?

Objectives Index

The Early Years Foundation Stage
Early Learning Goals: Problem Solving, Reasoning and Numeracy

National Curriculum
Key Stage 1

Key Stage 2

Primary Framework for Mathematics

Using and applying mathematics

Counting and understanding number

Knowing and using number facts

Calculating

Understanding shape

Measuring

Handling data

Page

References

Ainley, J, Pratt, D and Hansen, A (2006) Connecting engagement and focus in pedagogical task design. *British Educational Research Journal*, 32 (1), 23–38.

Amin, Z and Eng, KH (2003) *Basics in medical education*. London: World Scientific Publishing.

Anghilieri, J and Baron, S (1999) Playing with the materials of study: poleidoblocs. *Education, 3–13*, 27 (2), 57–64.

Askew, M, Brown, M, Rhodes, V, Wiliam, D and Johnson, D (1997a) *Effective teachers of numeracy: report of a study carried out for the Teacher Training Agency*. London: King's College, University of London.

Askew, M, Brown, M, Rhodes, V, Wiliam, D and Johnson, D (1997b) *Effective teachers of numeracy in primary schools: teachers' beliefs, practices and pupils' learning*. Paper presented at the British Educational Research Association Annual Conference, 11–15 September, University of York.

ATM (2003) *Young children learning mathematics*. Derby: ATM.

Aubrey, C (1997) *Mathematics teaching in the Early Years: an investigation of teachers' subject knowledge*. London: Falmer Press.

Ball, DL and Bass, H (2000) Interweaving content and pedagogy in teaching and learning to teach: knowing and using mathematics. In Boaler, J (ed.), *Multiple perspectives on the teaching and learning of mathematics*. Westport, CT: Ablex, pp83–104.

Ball, DL, Hill, HH and Bass, H (2005) Knowing mathematics for teaching: who knows mathematics well enough to teach third grade, and how can we decide? *American Mathematical Educator*, Fall, 14–46.

Baroody, AJ and Ginsburg, HP (1983) The effects of instruction on children's understanding of the 'equals' sign. *The Elementary School Journal*, 84 (2), 198–212.

Barrett, JE and Clemson, DH (1998) Analysing children's length strategies with two-dimensional tasks: what counts for length? In Berenson, SB, Dawkins, KR, Blanton, M, Coulombe, WN, Kolb, J, Norwood, K and Stiff, K (eds), *Proceedings of the 12th Annual North American Chapter of the International Group for the Psychology of Mathematics Education*. Columbus, OH: ERIC Clearinghouse for Science, Mathematics, and Environment Education, Vol. 1, pp321–7.

BBC News (2000) Mars probe canyon crash theory. http://news.bbc.co.uk/1/hi/sci/tech/593264.stm (accessed 6 January 2008).

BBC (2008) Average conditions: Cape Town, South Africa. www.bbc.co.uk/weather/world/city_guides/results.shtml?tt=TT000580 (accessed 3 January 2008).

Bills, L, Ainley, J and Wilson, K (2006) Modes of algebraic communication – moving from spreadsheets to standard notation. *For the Learning of Mathematics*, 26 (1), 41–7.

Carruthers, E and Worthington, M (2005) Making sense of mathematical graphics: the development of understanding abstract symbolism. *European Early Childhood Education Research Journal*, 13 (1), 57–79.

Cass, M, Cates, D, Jackson, C and Smith M. (2003) Effects of manipulative instruction on solving area and perimeter problems by students with learning disabilities. *Learning Disabilities Research and Practice*, 18 (2), 112–20.

Chakrabarti, DK (2004) *Indus civilization sites in India: new discoveries*. Mumbai: Marg Publications.

Clarke, B, Clarke, DM and Horne, M (2006) A longitudinal study of children's mental computation strategies. In Novotná, J, Moraová, H, Krátká, M and Stehlíková, N (eds), *Proceedings of the 30th Conference of the International Group for the Psychology of Mathematics Education*. Prague: PME, Vol. 2, pp329–36.

Clements, DH and Battista, MT (1992) Geometry and spatial reasoning. In Grouws, DA (ed.), *Handbook of research in mathematics teaching and learning*. New York: Macmillan, pp420–64.

Clements, DH, Battista, MT and Sarama, J (1998) Development of geometric and measurement ideas. In Lehrer, R and Chazan, D (eds), *Designing learning environments for developing understanding of geometry and space*. Hillsdale, NJ: Lawrence Erlbaum Associates, pp201–47.

Cole, C and Newson, G (1996) Primary children's views on using calculators in school. *Mathematics Education Review*, 7, January.

Davies, N, Connor, D and Spencer, N (2003) An international project for the development of data handling skills of teachers and pupils. *Journal of Applied Mathematics and Decision Sciences*, 7 (2), 75–83.

DfEE (1999) *The National Curriculum: handbook for primary teachers in England*. London: DfEE/QCA.

DfES (2001) *The framework for teaching mathematics and the approach to calculation: Unit 5*. London: DfES.

DfES (2004) *Every Child Matters: change for children*. London: DfES. Available from: www.everychildmatters.gov.uk/ (accessed 12 November 2007).

DfES (2006) *Primary Framework for Teaching Mathematics*. London: DfES.

DfES (2007a) *The Early Years Foundation Stage. Effective practice: observation, assessment and planning*. London: DfES. Available from: www.standards.dcsf.gov.uk/eyfs/resources/downloads/3_1_ep.pdf (accessed 14 January 2008).

DfES (2007b) *The Early Years Foundation Stage. Effective practice: outdoor learning*. London: DfES Publications.

DfES (2007c) *The Early Years Foundation Stage: setting the standards for learning, development and care for children from birth to five*. London: DfES.

Doerr, H (2006) Examining the tasks of teaching when using students' mathematical thinking. *Educational Studies in Mathematics*, 62 (1), 3–24.

Doerr, H and English, LD (2006) Middle grade teachers' learning through students' engagement with modeling tasks. *Journal of Mathematics Teacher Education*, 9 (1), 5–32.

Donaldson, J and Scheffler, A (2003) *The snail and the whale*. London: Macmillan Children's Books.

Dougherty, B and Slovin, H (2004) Generalised diagrams as a tool for young children's problem solving. In *Proceedings of the 28th Conference of the International Group for the Psychology of Mathematics Education*. Bergen, Norway: PME, Vol. 2, pp295–302.

Edwards, D (1991) Discourse and the development of understanding in the classroom. In Boyd-Barrett, O and Scanlon, E (eds), *Computers and learning*. Wokingham: Addison-Wesley.

English, L and Watters, JJ (2005) Mathematical modelling with 9-year-olds. In Chick, HL and Vincent, JL (eds), *Proceedings of the 29th Conference of the International group for the Psychology of Mathematics Education*. Melbourne: PME. Vol. 2, pp297–304.

Eyles, A (1999) Paying children to do their maths! *Primary Mathematics*, 2 (3).

Ferrara, F, Pratt, D and Robutti, O (2006) The role and uses of technology of algebra and calculus. In Gutiérrez, A and Boero, P (eds), *Handbook of research on the psychology of mathematics education*. Rotterdam: Sense Publishers, pp305–46.

Fischbein, E (1993) The theory of figural concepts. *Educational Studies in Mathematics*, 24 (2), 139 62.

Fischbein, E (1994) The interaction between the formal, the algorithmic and the intuitive components in a mathematical activity. In Biehler, R et al. (eds), *Didactics of mathematics as a scientific discipline*. Dordrecht: Reidel, pp231–45.

Fisher, C (2004) Multiplying and dividing decimals by powers of ten. www.onemathematicalcat.org/algebra_book/online_problems/mdd_powers_of_ten.htm (accessed 6 January 2008).

Foster, R (1997) It's that goat page! *Education 3–13*, 25 (1), 44–8.

French, D (2004) *Teaching and learning geometry: issues and methods in mathematical education*. London: Continuum.

Frobisher, L, Monaghan, J, Orton, A and Orton, J (1999) *Learning to teach number – a handbook for students and teachers in the primary school*. London: Stanley Thornes.

Fujita, T and Jones, K (2006) Primary trainee teachers' understanding of basic geometrical figures in Scotland. In Novotná, H, Moraová, H, Krátká, M and Stehlíková, N (eds), *Proceedings of the 30th Conference of the International Group for the Psychology of Mathematics Education*. Prague: PME, Vol. 3, pp129–36.

Furner, JM and Marinas, CA (2007) Geometry sketching software for elementary children: easy as 1, 2, 3. *Eurasia Journal of Mathematics, Science and Technology Education*, 3 (1), 83–91.

Fusion, K (1986) Teaching children to subtract by counting up. *Journal for Research in Mathematics Education*, 17 (3), 172–89.

Fusion, K (1992) Research on learning and teaching addition and subtraction of whole numbers. In Leinhardt, G, Putman, R and Hattrup, R (eds), *Analysis of arithmetic for mathematics teaching*. Hillsdale, NJ: Lawrence Erlbaum Associates, pp52–187.

Fusion, K and Willis, GB (1988) Subtracting by counting up: more evidence. *Journal for Research in Mathematics Education*, 19 (5), 402–20.

Galili, I (2001) Weight versus gravitational force: historical and educational perspectives. *International Journal of Science Education*, 23 (10), 1073–93.

Garrick, R (2002) *Pattern-making and pattern play in the nursery: special organisation*. Paper presented at the Annual Conference of the British Educational Research Association, University of Exeter, England, 12–14 September.

Gelman, R (1978) Counting in the preschooler: what does and does not develop. In RS Siegler (ed.), *Children's thinking: what develops?* Hillsdale, NJ: Erlbaum.

Gelman, R and Gallistel, CR (1978) *The child's understanding of number*. Cambridge, MA: Harvard University Press.

Gray, EM and Tall, DO (1994) Duality, ambiguity and flexibility: a proceptual view of simple arithmetic. *Journal for Research in Mathematics Education*, 26 (2), 115–41.

Greeno, JG (1980) Some examples of cognitive task analysis with instructional implications. In Snow, RE, Frederico, P and Montague, WE (eds), *Aptitude, learning and instruction, Vol. 2: Cognitive process analysis of learning and problem-solving*. Hillsdale, NJ: Lawrence Erlbaum Associates, pp1–21.

Groves, S and Stacey, K (1996) Redefining early number concepts through calculator use. In Mulligan, J and Mitchelmore, M (eds), *Children's number learning*. Adelaide: Australian Association of Mathematics Teachers, pp205–26.

Hansen, A (ed.) (2005) *Children's errors in mathematics*. Exeter: Learning Matters.

Hansen, A (2007) Using models and images to support children's mathematical thinking. In Drews, D and Hansen, A (eds), *Using resources to support mathematical thinking*. Exeter: Learning Matters.

Hasegawa, J (1997) Concept formation of triangles and quadrilaterals in second grade. *Educational Studies in Mathematics*, 32, 157–79.

Heirdsfield, A and Cooper, TJ (2004) Factors affecting the process of proficient mental addition and subtraction: case studies of flexible and inflexible computers. *Journal of Mathematical Behavior*, 23 (4), 443–63.

Hembree, R and Dessart, DJ (1992) Research on calculators in mathematics education. In Fey, JT (ed.), *Calculators in mathematics education: 1992 yearbook of the National Council of Teachers of Mathematics*. Reston, VA: NCTM, pp22–31.

Hershkowitz, R (1990) Psychological aspects of learning geometry. In Nesher, P and Kilpatrick, J (eds), *Mathematics and cognition*. Cambridge: Cambridge University Press, pp70–95.

Hershkowitz, R, Ben-Chaim, D, Hoyles, C, Lappan, G, Mitchelmore, M and Vinner, S (1990) Psychological aspects of learning geometry. In Nesher, P and Kilpatrick, J (eds), *Mathematics and cognition: a research synthesis by the International Group for the Psychology of Mathematics Education*. Cambridge: Cambridge University Press, pp70–95.

Hughes, M (1986) *Children and number: difficulties in learning mathematics*. Oxford: Blackwell.

Jones, I and Pratt, D (2005) Three utilities for the equal sign. In Chick, HL and Vincent, JL (eds), *Proceedings of the 29th Conference of the International Group for the Psychology of Mathematics Education*. Melbourne: PME, Vol. 3, pp185–92.

Jones, I and Pratt, D (2006) Connecting the equals sign. *International Journal of Computers for Mathematical Learning*, 11 (3), 301–25.

Jones, K (2003) Research bibliography: four-function calculators. *MicroMath*, 19 (1), 33–4.

Kafai, YB, Franke, ML, Ching, CC and Shih, JC (1998) Game design as an interactive learning environment for fostering students' and teachers' mathematical enquiry. *International Journal of Computers for Mathematical Learning*, 3(2), 149–84.

Koshy, V and Murray, J (2002) *Unlocking numeracy*. London: David Fulton.

Lehrer, R, Jenkins, M and Osana, H (1998) Longitudinal study of children's reasoning about space and geometry. In Lehrer, R and Chazan, D (eds), *Designing learning environments for developing understanding of geometry and space*. Hillsdale, NJ: Lawrence Erlbaum Associates, pp137–67.

Lesh, R. and English, LD (2005) Trends in the evolution of models and modelling perspectives on mathematical learning and problem solving. In Chick, HL and Vincent, JL (eds), *Proceedings 29th Conference of the International Group for the Psychology of Mathematics Education*. Melbourne: PME, Vol. 1 (1), pp192–6.

Lesh, R. and Zawojewski, JS (2007). Problem solving and modeling. In F Lester (Ed.) *Second Handbook of research on mathematics teaching and learning.* Greenwich, CT: Information Age Publishing.

Margolinas, C, Coulange, L and Bessot, A (2005) What can the teacher learn in the classroom? *Educational Studies in Mathematics*, 59 (1–3), 205–34.

Mokros, J and Russell, SJ (1995) Children's concepts of average and representative-ness. *Journal for Research in Mathematics Education*, 26 (1), pp20–39.

Montague-Smith, A (1997) *Mathematics in nursery education*. London: David Fulton.

Morris, H (2001) Issues raised by testing trainee primary teachers' mathematical knowledge. *Mathematics Education Research Journal*, 3, 37–47.

Mullet, E and Gervais, H (1990) Distinction between the concepts of weight and mass in high school students. *International Journal of Science Education*, 12 (2), 217–26.

Munn, P (1997) Children's beliefs about counting. In Thompson, I (ed.), *Teaching and learning early number*. Buckingham: Open University Press.

Murray, J (2003) Mental mathematics. In Koshy, V, Ernest, P and Casey, R (eds), *Mathematics for primary teachers*. London: Routledge.

National Numeracy Strategy (1999) *Primary Framework for literacy and mathematics*. London: NNS.

Nickson, M (2004) *Teaching and learning mathematics: a guide to recent research and its applications*. 2nd edition. London: Continuum.

Noss, R (1987) Children's learning of geometrical concepts through Logo. *Journal for Research in Mathematics Education*, 18 (5), 343–62.

Ofsted (2001) *The National Numeracy Strategy: the second year. An evaluation by HMI*. Available from: www.ofsted.gov.uk (accessed 14 August 2007).

Onslow, B (2002) *Esso family math (Grades 2–5)*, 3rd edition. Cited in Sauer, R (2002) *Estimation*. Ontario: GTK Press.

Ouseley, H and Lane, J (2006) *Early Years Foundation Stage: response to the consultation on a single quality framework for services to children from birth to five. Every Child Matters: change for children*. London: Blink. Available from www.blink.org.uk/docs/EYFS_HO_AN_JL_July%2006.pdf (accessed 12 November 2007).

Platz, D (2004) Challenging young children through simple sorting and classifying: a developmental approach. *Education*, Fall. Available from: http://findarticles.com/p/articles/mi_qa3673/is_200410/ai_n9429975/pg_1 (accessed 13 January 2008).

PNS (2006) *Renewing the Primary Framework for Mathematics Guidance Paper: oral and mental work in mathematics*. Available from: www.standards.dfes.gov.uk/primaryframeworks/mathematics/Papers/oral_and_mental_activity/ (accessed 8 January 2008).

PNS (2007a) *Guidance Paper – Calculation*. Available at: www.standards.dfes.gov.uk/primaryframeworks/mathematics/Papers/Calculation/ (accessed 10 January 2008).

PNS (2007b) *The use of calculators in the teaching and learning of mathematics*. Available at: www.standards.dfes.gov.uk/primaryframeworks/mathematics/Papers/Calculators/ (accessed 10 January 2008.

Pound, L (1999) *Supporting mathematical development in the early years*. Buckingham: Open University Press.

QCA (1999) *Mental calculation strategies*. London: QCA.

QCA (2007) See http://www.qca.org.uk/eara/189.asp.

QCA (2008) *Key Stage 2 assessment and reporting arrangements 2008*. Available from www.qca.org.uk/eara/documents/KS2_v07aw-2.pdf (accessed 10 January 2008).

Raiker, A (2007) Assessment for learning. In Jacques, K and Hyland, R (eds), *Professional studies: primary and early years*. 3rd edition. Exeter: Learning Matters, pp46–59.

Reys, RE, Suydam, MN and Lindquist, MM (1995) *Helping children learn mathematics*. Needham Heights: Allyn & Bacon.

Reys, RE, Lindquist, MM, Lambdin, DV, Smith, NL and Suydam, MN (2006) *Helping children learn mathematics*. 8th edition. Boston: John Wiley & Sons.

Robinson, A (2007) *The story of measurement*. London: Thames & Hudson.

Rodrigues, S (1994) Data handling in the primary classroom: children's perception of the purpose of graphs. *Research in Science Education*, 24 (1), 280–6.

Rowland, T, Martyn, S, Barber, P and Heal, C (2001) Investigating the mathematics subject matter knowledge of pre-service elementary school teachers. In van den Heuvel-Panhuizen, M. (ed.), *Proceedings of the 23rd Conference of the International Group for the Psychology of Mathematics Education*. Utrecht: Freudenthal Institute, Utrecht University, Vol. 4, pp121–8.

Rudduck, J and Flutter, J (2004) *How to improve your school: giving pupils a voice*. London: Continuum Press.

Ruthven, K (1998) The use of mental, written and calculator strategies of numerical computation by upper primary pupils within a 'calculator-aware' number curriculum. *British Educational Research Journal*, 24 (1), 21–42.

Saads, S and Davis, G (1997) Spacial abilities, van Hiele levels and language used in three dimensional geometry. *Proceedings of the 22nd Conference of the International Group for the Psychology of Mathematics Education*. Lahti, Finland: PME, Vol. 4. pp104–11.

Scheuneman, JD, Camara, WJ, Cascallar, AS, Wendler, C and Lawrence, I (2002) Calculator access, use, and type in relation to performance on the SAT I: Reasoning Test in mathematics. *Applied Measurement in Education*, 15 (1), 95–112.

Schlessinger Media (2004) *Zeros. Multiplying and dividing by 10, 100 and 1000*. Available at: www.libraryvideo.com/guides/v6441.pdf (accessed 6 January 2008).

Schliemann, A, Brizuela, B, Carraher, D, Earnest, D, Goodrow, A, Lara-Roth, S and Peled, I (2003) Algebra in elementary school. In Pateman, NA, Dougherty, BJ and Zilliox, J (eds), *Proceedings of the 27th Conference of the International Group for the Psychology of Mathematics Education held jointly with the 25th Conference of PME-NA*. Hawai'i: PME, Vol. 4, pp127–34.

Schmandt-Besserat, D (1999) *The history of counting*. New York: Harper Collins.

Shulman, L (1986) Those who understand: knowledge growth in teaching. *Educational Researcher*, 15 (2), 4–14.

Shulman, L (1987) *Knowledge and teaching: Foundations of the new reform*. Harvard Education Review, 57, 1–22.

Sigler, L (2003) *Fibonacci's Liber Abaci: Leonardo Pisano's book of calculation*. New York: Springer-Verlag.

Smidt, S (2005) *Observing, assessing and planning for children in the Early Years*. London: Routledge.

Streefland, L (1991) *Fractions in realistic mathematics education*. Dordrecht: Kluwer Academic.

Streefland, L (1993) Fractions: a realistic approach. In Carpenter, TP, Fennema, E and Romberg, TA (eds), *Rational numbers: an integration of research*. Hillsdale, NJ: Lawrence Erlbaum Associates.

TDA (2007a) *Professional standards for teachers: qualified teacher status*. London: TDA.

TDA (2007b) Editorial. *tdaNews*, May.

TDA (2008) *Subject knowledge booster courses*. Available from: www.tda.gov.uk/Recruit/thetrainingprocess/youroptionsinfull/pretrainingcourses/subjectknowledge boostecourses. aspx (accessed 11 January 2008).

Thompson, I (1999) *Teaching and learning early number*. Buckingham: Open University Press.

Thompson, I (2003), *Enhancing primary mathematics teaching*. London: Open University Press.

Tobin, K (1987) The role of wait time in higher cognitive level learning. *Review of Educational Research* (ERIC Clearinghouse on Reading and Communication Skills), 57 (1), 69–95.

Vandersteen, G (2002) Children's own methods of recording number. *Mathematics in School*, November, pp2–8.

Wallace, P (2005) Blending instructional design principles with computer game design: the development of Descartes' Cove. *Proceedings of the Association for the Advancement of Computing in Education, Educational Multimedia and Hypermedia, Montreal, Canada*. Chesapeake, VA: AACE, pp402–7.

Watson, J (2007) The role of cognitive conflict in developing students' understanding of average. *Educational Studies in Mathematics*, 65 (1), 21–47.

Watson, J and Moritz, JB (2000) The longitudinal development of understanding of average. *Mathematical Thinking and Learning*, 2 (1 & 2), 11–50.

Wilson, K, Ainley, J and Bills, L (2005) Spreadsheets, pedagogic strategies and the evolution of meaning for variable. In Chick, HL and Vincent, JL (eds), *Proceedings of the 29th Annual Conference of the International Group for the Psychology of Mathematics Education*. Melbourne: PME, Vol. 4, pp321–8.

Wood, E (2007) Reconceptualising child-centred education: contemporary directions in policy, theory and practice in early childhood. *FORUM: For Promoting 3–19 Comprehensive Education*, 49 (1), 119–34.

Worthington, M and Carruthers, E (2003) Research uncovers children's creative mathematical thinking. *Primary Mathematics* (Mathematics Association), 7 (3), 21–5.

Worthington, M and Carruthers, E (2005) *The art of children's mathematics: the power of visual representation*. Paper presented at Roehampton University's 'Art in Early Childhood: Creativity, Collaboration, Communication' Conference, 7–9 July.

Wu, H (2002) *On the teaching of fractions*. Berkley, CA: University of California. Available at: http://math.berkeley.edu/~wu/EMI2a.pdf (accessed 1 November 2006).

Yackel, E and Cobb, P (1996) Sociomathematical norms, argumentation, and autonomy in mathematics. *Journal for Research in Mathematics Education*, 27 (4), 458–77.

Index